PRAISE

"Girl, Boss Up!" is the book every young woman needs in order to stay focused and succeed in the corporate world and in life! Written like a favorite auntie speaking to her niece, Karen Hoskin's story is riveting, entertaining, and sprinkled with words of wisdom and mentorship throughout her journey. This book is a refreshing must read!

— KIM BROOKS, *Bestselling Author and Women Empowerment Speaker*

Minorities still face many barriers in all professional fields, but Information Technology, Cybersecurity and Certified Public Accounting are particularly lacking women, especially women of color. Karen's true stories connect with our hearts, and her principles give us real practical guidance in being authentic at work.

— ROSE KWON, *IT Digital and Customer Services and former CIO NAFTA at Mercedes-Benz USA*

"Girl, Boss Up!" Is a great read for young adults seeking success in the corporate world. It teaches practical lessons on how to navigate the workplace and inspires readers to persevere in your purpose.

— PASTOR ANDRÉ BUTLER, *Lead Pastor, Faith Xperience Church*

The more things change, the more they stay the same. Reading about Karen Hoskin's first corporate role felt like I was reading my diary, although there were almost 40 years between our experiences. My biggest qualm about being Black in corporate was feeling like everyone had access to information I wasn't privy to, and this book feels like the secret manual I've been missing. Karen shares her own experiences in a way that is candid and relatable. I see myself throughout the pages. Her story is a beautiful reminder of the resilience of Black women while providing a peek behind the curtain at all the things we endure as we climb the corporate ladder. The career lessons and principles she shares are timeless and could be helpful for anyone of any background who is early in their career. I can't thank her enough for writing this. This book is GUARANTEED to bring the BOSS out of you!

— TIARA JONES, *MSM*

"Girl Boss Up!" is the perfect, inspirational text for today's next generation. In the book, author Karen Hoskin gives eloquent words of wisdom for young women who may be entering the workforce by using her own experiences in rising the ranks of corporate America as an accountant. This book encourages girls of all ages to go after their dreams no matter the obstacles they may face because in the end the achievements will outweigh the challenges. Hoskin is a living testimony that going after your goals in life like she did in becoming a Certified Public Accountant can all be achieved with hard work and faith.

— VERONICA JOHNSON, *MLIS, Journalist, Freelance Music Writer and Archivist*

"Girl, Boss Up!" author takes you on a captivating journey through her experience in corporate America as a professional Black woman. The authenticity of lessons learned and shared are an excellent guide for the next generation of professional women in general and professional Black women. "Girl, Boss Up!" is an absolute must read!

— T. MOON, *Senior Facilities Service Representative Fortune 500 Firm*

Girl, BOSS UP!

Seven Principles to Empower You in the Workplace

KAREN "CORPORATE AUNTIE K" **HOSKIN**, CISM , CPA, CAMS

Girl, Boss Up!

Copyright 2020 by Karen Hoskin, CPA, CISM, CAMS

All rights reserved. This book or parts thereof may not be reproduced in any form, stored in a retrieval system or transmitted in any form by any means – electronic, mechanical, photocopy, recording or otherwise – without written permission of the publisher, except as provided by United States of America copyright law.

Published in the United States

By Paulirma, Limited Liability Company

Novi, Michigan

DEDICATION

In loving memory of my parents,
Paul and Irma Lee Hoskin

CONTENTS

1. Starting Out in Corporate America 3
2. Being Let Go - Fired 19
3. Horrible Bosses 27
4. The Unemployment Season 38
5. 25 Keys for How Not to Get Fired 44
6. I Hate My Job 47
7. Negotiating Salaries 50
8. Being a Woman in Corporate America 53
9. Being Black in Corporate America 55
10. How to Identify Why You Are Here and Your Purpose 60
11. Girl Boss 75
12. 7 Principles to Empower You in the Workplace 83

    Principle # 1 – Six Habits of Powerful People 83

    Principle # 2 – How to Leverage Your Personality 88

    Principle #3 – How to Cultivate Your Strengths 93

    Principle # 4 - How to Crack the People Puzzle &
                   Manage Conflict 97

    Principle # 5 – How to Engage Your Personal Brand 111

    Principle # 6 – How to Conquer Your Blind Spots 116

    Principle # 7 – How to Obtain the Optimal Work-life Balance 119

FOREWORD

Reading the first few chapters of "Girl, Boss Up!" brought up nostalgic memories of the day Karen walked into our office to lead my team of security professionals through the remediation steps of critical corporate audit findings after our manager went on medical leave. Karen was looking sharp in her pink suit and exuded a confident demeanor and a big smile that conveyed the confidence of a go-getter. She did not waste time getting down to business to coalesce support amongst the management team and subject matter experts for the audit findings remediation plan. During our one-on-one, she stated that she needed my help and guidance and made it clear that I would be in the trenches with her. That eventually meant working long hours together to unravel the knotty audit findings. Even in the thick of things in stressful situations, her laughter and words of faith kept us going. She did not waste time showing everyone that she was the new boss in charge and would not back down from challenges on her approach from other senior and technical colleagues. She would negotiate when she felt there was a need to but always ready to fight to ensure that the team realized the need for the remediation plan to resolve the audit finding sustainably. This book is filled with stories of trials and triumphs, and it will be a valuable read to those (male and female) who feel stuck in their career or work situations and begin to despair. They will learn from the numerous life lessons and experiences that Karen highlighted as visible nuggets throughout this book. As Karen stated in the book, set goals for every job you take, and be ready to learn and grow from the inherent life lessons. Karen and I worked hard, laughed hard, made tremendous progress, and had fun through it all. I admire Karen for her ability to control a chaotic situation and establish credibility among technical and security experts. But one thing that endeared me to her is her strong faith and beliefs. It was amazing to read in her book how she found her faith in God and to testify that she is a true believer that relies on her faith in all she does.

Thank you, Karen, for giving us a glimpse into your experience and how it has shaped the "Boss Lady" you have become.

Abraham O. Okomanyi
M.Eng., M.I.S.M., P.M.P, TOGAF9, CISSP, CCSP

ACKNOWLEDGEMENTS

I would like to thank God for giving me this idea to share with all of you my years of experience in many workplace roles and responsibilities.

Thank you Michele Tate, Jillian Govan, Veronica Johnson, Tina Hewlett and Leah Olajide for all of your creativity, editorial comments and strategic guidance.

And thanks to my pastor, Andre Butler of Faith Xperience Church for all of your support, teachings and encouragement.

INTRODUCTION

I had just returned from a work assignment as an interim Information Security Officer in Atlanta and coming down from the high of my success. For the first time in my career, I was sitting in meetings with presidents and senior executives from around the world and advising them on their company's next strategic moves. This was a dream and the kind of work I've always wanted to do. It only took me 30 years to get here. As I leaned back in my chair, I thought of all the lessons I've learned in the process.

I thought about the experience that led me to that moment. Then I thought of who might benefit from my experiences. This book, "Girl, Boss Up!" is the book I wish I had to guide me in my career. It would have saved me plenty of knocks on the head and given me the boost I needed to succeed in my career. So, I wrote this book as a guide for your journey in the workplace. I hope to save you from making the mistakes I made, while also giving you the wisdom and foresight to catapult your career.

"Girl, Boss Up!" is my story. It's my lessons learned. I hope that as you read, you will discover the tools you need to hit success faster than I did. I address the common question of "why am I here?" and provide seven principles to enhance your power in the workplace.

So, come on this journey with me and learn how to have the successful career you always dreamed of.

Girl, BOSS UP!

1
Starting Out in Corporate America

It's official! The offer letter came in the mail today! I thought to myself 'I would soon begin my career in public accounting as a staff auditor.' I had just finished my degree in Business Administration, majoring in Accounting and the last two years of college had been difficult. The university's business school was tough and by junior year, many students had changed majors because they could not pass the accounting exams. I can still remember my accounting instructor Dr. Hern, a slender brown-haired khaki pants enthusiast who loved the sound of his own voice. Among the students, he was known as "The Terminator." His midterm exam left many questioning their career path. I was getting tired and was disappointed about picking up C's along the way. However, one professor's advice stood out to me. He said, "Just finish." It made sense; it is more important to finish the degree than to get perfect grades. I stopped obsessing over obtaining A's and B's and finished my degree.

It is more important to finish the degree than to get perfect grades.

During my senior year, one of the Big Four firms (formerly the Big

Eight) came to recruit on Wayne State University's campus. They were nicknamed the Big Four because they were the four largest professional services networks in the world. It was an elite group of individuals selected to work there. They were particularly known all over the world for their accounting services. They gave me the red-carpet treatment during the interview, so I was extremely excited about working for them. I thought, 'wow what a dream come true! This black girl from Detroit overcame all odds, graduated, and landed a prestigious position in corporate America.'

It was my first day of work and I could hardly wait to start the day. I entered the office, ready to take on the world. At 8:30 am I attended a Welcome meeting with some of the firm's senior partners and met the other new hires. I walked into the Welcome meeting. I canvassed the room checking out all the newbies. Of the 25 new hires in the room, I counted eight women, and two people of color. Jasmine, the only other black woman in the room would prove to be a close ally. We did a round table of introductions, but when it came time to mingle, Jasmine and I naturally gravitated to each other. She was a little older than me and transferred from our sister firm in Jamaica. We were both nervous and relieved to connect with someone who looked like us. Once the Welcome meeting was over, I returned to my cube and received my first work assignment.

My first audit was examining the financial records of one of the Big 3 automotive companies. I was nervous, but I had to put on my "big girl pants" and work. When I walked through the shiny glass doors and entered the lobby, I was met by my supervisor and another member of the team. It was routine in public accounting for the rookie to be accompanied by a senior auditor and seasoned staff auditor. The senior auditor was a guy named Sean, a pudgy, blue eyed cynic in his early thirties. Sean had been with the company for more than five years. And he had been on this audit engagement his entire career. Fast track colleagues were promoted to manager within four to five years of joining the firm. It was his sixth year and he expected to be promoted during his last performance review, but it did not happen. He oozed entitlement and loved to ruin a great day with his displeasure and apathy. It was clear that learning from him was going to be a challenge.

As my supervisor, he was supposed to show me the ropes. You can imagine how that went. Sean provided no context as to how to approach my assignment. Getting my questions answered was like pulling teeth. He made it noticeably clear that he did not want to work with me by rolling his eyes and taking deep sighs when I approached him. Besides introducing me to the client on the first day, he was no help. It was up to me to sink or swim. I remember walking calmly into the bathroom, shutting the stall door behind me and sobbing silently on my lunch break. After I had a good cry, I looked in the mirror, pulled myself together and went back to work. I wanted to quit. This work experience was not the dream I had imagined. It was a nightmare! And what made things worse was that I had to spend 11 hours a day with these guys. When I went to work, it was dark and when I came home, it was dark.

My experience reminded me of the film "The Firm" starring Tom Cruise. It came out in 1993, several years after my work experience at this company. In this movie Tom's character Mitch, had just graduated from law school. They wined and dined him just like my firm did with me. He passed the bar and the company celebrated him. Mitch thought he had made the best decision of his life and that his new co-workers were his family. I started to realize, maybe this was what I thought during my interview process. Then one day, Mitch learned that the firm had mob ties. It was not the wonderful place he thought it to be. The truth was that the firm was complicit in tax fraud and money laundering. Things were going downhill fast. Then he learns four associates had mysteriously died. Mitch's life was in jeopardy. He was scared and on the run. He had to figure out how to implicate the firm without losing his life.

As I watched that movie, I felt Mitch's pain. I could relate so much to his experience. No one had tried to physically kill me, but I did feel like I was on the run. I can still feel the chills. I felt like I was watching my life relived on the big screen. He was in a law firm and I was in public accounting.

I needed to remember why I started. I needed inspiration to get me through this season. I wanted to be like my idol, the late Marie Farrell-Donaldson. She was the first black female Certified Public Accountant (CPA) in the state of Michigan. I later read in Ebony magazine that companies refused to hire her, although her credentials were outstanding. So, Marie started her own public accounting firm. During that era, there were very few black professionals in public accounting and very few female Certified Public Accountants. She became the first Black, the first woman and first CPA to hold the position of auditor general for the city of Detroit. Every time she spoke at Wayne State, I was there. The year I graduated; Marie was awarded as Wayne State's Outstanding Alumni. I attended the award ceremony. She gave an eloquently charged speech and everyone applauded. I contemplated going up to speak to her, and as I thought about it, I could feel the invisible sweat on my forehead. I slowly got up from my chair to go stand in the now long line. I waited patiently for my turn. I took a deep breath and extended my hand. She shook my hand and smiled. I don't remember the details of our conversation probably because I was so nervous to meet her. She inspired me although she never knew it. Thinking of her reminded me of what I was aiming for.

I couldn't quit although I would have liked to. I had only been there a month and I had no idea where I would go. I did not know about job recruiters. Back then there was no such thing as Career Builder.com or Indeed.com. Google was not even a thing. Overtime, what I found is that you cannot keep running from one job to the next just because it is uncomfortable or there are some challenges. If you do this, these uncomfortable moments and challenges will show up at the next work assignment.

You cannot keep running from one job to the next just because it is uncomfortable or there are some challenges. If you do this, these uncomfortable moments and challenges will show up at the next work assignment.

So, here's what you must remember:
- *Don't be afraid.*
- *Uncomfortable moments are temporary.*
- *Grow in this space; every work assignment comes with life lessons that you can grow from.*

What I needed was a mentor. I did not have one, but I had Jasmine. When the audit was over, I went back to the office and Jasmine was there. Jasmine was not naïve like me. She had been around a while and was seasoned. She brought to my attention how "the boys club" were given all the best work assignments. They were always given the jobs with high visibility while we were given the leftovers. Jasmine and I did not fit the cookie cutter representation that the company wanted to promote. This is not something we could openly express with the powers that be, so we would express our frustrations in the ladies' room. She taught me to always look for feet under the stalls to make sure no one heard us talking. In the ladies' room was where we shared our pain. It was where we discussed the racial hatred we were experiencing day in and day out. What did I expect from Corporate America? It certainly was not this.

At least my personal life was going well. I was dating a great guy. I was having fun on the weekends with Robert. We would go to concerts, dinner, and amusement parks. We met during our Sophomore year of college. He was studying optometry and I was studying business administration. We connected over contemporary jazz and sports. Life was busy but we always made time for each other. Spending time with Robert was a great distraction from my work woes.

After finishing the awful audit with my supervisor Sean, I was finally able to relieve myself of the assignment and him. I received my new assignment with a different supervisor in Saline, Michigan. One day myself and my new supervisor left the client's office and went to lunch at a restaurant called "Genitti's Hole-in the Wall." This place had the best alfredo pasta. We ate from mix-matched plates, and drank beverages out of jelly jars. This audit was different. I was so relieved to work with kind people, that I laughed infectiously. We still worked long hours, but at least I was having fun. I received a great performance review, which was exciting. I was hopeful.

Setting Goals

The firm must have heard my cry for a mentor. It was early in my career and I needed guidance. Thankfully, the partners introduced a program that matched new hires with senior leaders, and it was just what I needed. I was paired up with Wendy, a short, confident, and commanding lady who happened to be African American. She was also the only female partner in the firm. To see someone who looked like me, who was both a woman and African American was astonishing; this was unheard at the time. I would often ask myself, 'how did she ever make it to partner?'

When I met her in her office, I remember being uncomfortable and nervous sitting in her presence. I don't remember most of our conversation, but I do remember one question she asked. Looking me straight in the eye, matter-of-factly she said, "Karen, what do you want out of this job?" No one had ever asked me that. I didn't even think to set a goal or expectation for being there. However, I did have an answer. I said, "I want to be certified." Boom! That was it! I did not want to hang around the firm for long, but I wanted to be a certified public accountant (CPA). That meant I needed to stay at least two years to meet the work requirement to be a CPA and pass the license exam. This was an "aha" moment for me! From that day on, I decided to set goals for every job I took. I had a vision now and for the first time, I was okay with my job choice. The environment was still tough, but I kept my eye on the prize.

Set goals for every job you take.

What is Going On?

A few months had gone by and I wasn't feeling well. I had a blaring headache, my back was hurting, and I was restless. I was starting to think those long work hours were catching up with me. Nonetheless, I made an appointment to see my doctor. When I arrived at his office, he began to examine me and ask questions.

"Describe your symptoms. When did you first start to feel this way? How long have you been having these headaches?"

After the exam, I sat there staring off into space, waiting for my results. I was a little concerned because I had no idea what could have been wrong with me. I was taking my vitamins. I was in pretty good shape, I thought. Maybe I was just stressed. Finally, I heard a knock on the door and the doctor entered. He looked at me with a smile and said, "You're going to be just fine. You're pregnant." It was as if his words echoed in my head a few times before I could respond. Pregnant was not the diagnosis I was expecting. I could not believe what I was hearing. I sat there quietly, still processing the news as the doctor filled out my prescriptions and the nurse handed me a sample of the mommy vitamins. 'Good thing I had taken the day off,' I thought. My mind was swarming with questions. 'How am I going to take care of a baby?' 'Who's going to watch the baby while I work?' 'How am I supposed to be a mom working in this high pressure male dominant work environment?'

In the 80s, you didn't just pop up pregnant and unmarried. There were negative consequences. You could be publicly shamed or worse, lose your job. I was overwhelmed by the thought of telling my employer. However, before I could even think about that, I had to tell my boyfriend first.

It was date night, and Robert was coming to pick me up. I did not mention my doctor's appointment when he called. I figured this is the kind of thing you share in person. The entire day I had not been able to think about anything else but telling him this news. When we sat down to dinner, I mulled over how to say it. I thought I'd ease into the conversation of my doctor's visit and go from there.

"Did I tell you I went to the doctor's office today?" I said.

"No, what's going on?"

I wasn't sure how to phrase it, so I just came right out and said it.

"I'm pregnant."

Robert's whole face dropped. "What do you mean you're pregnant?"

I'm not sure I heard much else after that. It was as if his words spewed at me like tiny daggers and landed into the pit of my stomach. Somewhere in the middle of his rant, I came to. He started rattling off his plans of moving to Boston to pursue his advanced degree. It was during that moment that I realized he had no intentions of sticking around. Reality was kicking in fast, showing me that I had wasted the past two years of my life in this relationship. Even though I did not want to grieve over it, I did. I tried to be strong, but it knocked the wind out of me. I had two new realities in front of me: I was single and I was also a single parent.

Adulting hits differently when you're having a baby. I was an emotional wreck and needed some support. I told my four sisters first and then I would tell my dad. 'How was I going to tell my dad his baby girl was pregnant and unmarried?' I thought. Telling him was probably the hardest thing I had to do. I was embarrassed and did not want to disappoint him, but I needed my family. Thankfully, my sisters and dad were incredibly supportive.

A Life Changing Moment

Although I was relieved to have family support, I still needed some advice. I thought to myself, 'How was I supposed to tell my employer I'm pregnant? Was I going to lose my job over this?' I had no friends with experience in this area, and no one in my family had ever worked in corporate America. It's as if heaven knew I needed a friend. Right there, in the office stood a pregnant woman with dark straight hair, a petite frame, and the belly the size of a basketball. She was about eight months pregnant. She had a pleasant countenance and an infectious smile that was inviting. We had never really talked before, just a polite "hi" in passing or a quick wave on the way to the copy room. Although I didn't know her very well, there was something about her that intrigued me. She was well known in the office as a do-gooder in the community and had an esteemed reputation for being a guest on Good Morning America where she shared her missionary work in South America. I was just as impressed with her as my colleagues and thought she'd make a great friend.

On that day, I decided I was going to ask her to lunch. I figured if anyone could advise me on how to be pregnant in corporate America, it was her. I was hesitant at first because I thought it might be awkward to ask. However, when I finally built up the courage, I was relieved that she accepted. I was so nervous from the time we left the office. I was preparing to confide in someone I barely knew about something so personal, but at the same time, I could hardly wait to get it off my chest. As the waitress left our table, I asked Margaret how she was feeling and when her baby was due. She shared her due date and that she would be going on maternity leave soon. She asked me how work was going. I told her it was okay. I sat across from her, feeling as if she and I were the only people in the room. I nursed my water for a while, trying to decide where and when I'd share my news. I was sure Margaret was wondering why I asked her out to lunch in the first place. I finally spilled the beans.

"I'm pregnant," I said softly. I felt uneasy as I waited for her response. She looked at me with assuring confidence and said,

"Karen, what are you believing God to do about your situation?"

I wasn't very religious at the time and wasn't sure what she meant by that. But I was relieved to have someone to confide in. Her response was like a call to action. As I pushed past the tears, she advised that I should make an appointment with the HR department to tell them my news. She told me not to worry, and she began to pray for me. She said,

"Dear God, help my new friend Karen. Comfort her and lead her now. In Jesus name,
Amen."

Near the end of lunch, she gave me her number and told me that I could call her at anytime. I left our conversation feeling lighter. Margaret had prayed for me and said everything was going to be alright.

I finally requested a meeting with the manager of HR. He welcomed me into his office, and I sat down. We started off with some light chatting, and I thanked him for taking the time to meet with me. He asked how I was doing and how I liked the firm. I shared the latest job I worked on and that it was going well.

"So, what brings you into today?" he asked.

It felt like a loud silence. I collected my thoughts for a moment, then told him that I was pregnant. In my mind, I already prepared myself for a negative response and I felt I was going to be terminated. I couldn't understand why my colleague Margaret was so certain that things would work in my favor. I thought, 'was it because of the prayers that she prayed?' I was holding onto my seat waiting for what seemed like forever for him to respond. Finally, he responded with, "Congratulations!" I cried tears of relief. In that field and in those times, it was a social stigma to be pregnant and unmarried. Although I still had challenges ahead, I was relieved to have this part behind me.

These days, I was thinking a lot more about God because of Margaret. She often told me that she was praying for me. She provided shining moments of hope to my days. Her caring and supportive words made me want to know God more. Then, I had this thought. Why don't I just go to church? So that Sunday, I did. I felt a little weird walking in because this was only the second time I had been to church in years. I didn't want to sit close to the front and was glad the usher directed me to a middle aisle seat. It wasn't long after I sat down that I was overcome with emotion. A pastor invited us to come down for prayer, and I went. I had been through so much in the last month; a breakup, workplace challenges and feeling alone. I was so emotional. Although things were better, I still felt like something was missing, and I desperately needed to feel like myself again. When I got to the front, the pastor led us in a prayer. The prayer went like this:

"God, change me. Jesus, come into my life."

Then something new happened. I felt a peace like I had never felt before. It felt like a giant weight lifted off me. That peace stayed with me. After that experience, I started reading my bible and learning about God. I somehow knew that God was with me. This was the greatest thing I could've done.

It was a beautiful spring day when I headed into the office. A lot of colleagues were there because the summer was the slow work season which also meant a lot of cubes were taken. I decided to take the staircase up to our other floor to see if I could find a seat there. As I walked toward the window in the stairwell, I started experiencing something horrible. It felt like an outside force was physically pulling me toward the window trying to entice me to jump. I was puzzled and afraid as I tried to figure out what this was and why was it happening. I had never thought of committing suicide before, so I was trying to figure out the source. While I tried to figure out what was happening, I started backing away from the window. I was frightened by the entire experience. I hurried up the staircase to find a cube where I could calm myself.

This suicide episode taught me something: we should focus our attention on the good things in our lives and be grateful. We should not waste our time worrying about bad things that could happen. Instead, focus on the good things in your life that are already happening and the future good things that can happen. My key takeaways were to value life and to value being a mother.

> ***Don't waste your time worrying about bad things that could happen. Instead, focus on the good things in your life that are already happening. And the future good things that can happen.***

I was holding fast to the goal I had to become a CPA and that meant passing the CPA exam. I also came to know that being a CPA was a highly coveted certification and obtaining it could open many doors of opportunity. I decided to go for it and prepare.

It was the month of May, which meant it was time to sit for the CPA exam. This exam was the singular most challenging exam of its kind and was often believed to be harder to pass than the law bar. The exam had four parts and it required that you achieve a passing score of at least 75% for each part to have successfully passed the entire exam. My goal was to pass the exam before I left the firm, and I was determined to do so.

In preparing for the exam, I spent 20 or more hours a week over several months studying. I had a huge commercial exam book, 500 pages thick, with exam questions at the end of each chapter to help me prepare. I spent many days and nights studying. You can imagine my disappointment when I received my scores in the mail only to find that I failed every section. All that studying and I had nothing to show for it. I felt exasperated. Somehow, I had to get over it, because at the end of the day, passing this exam was still my goal.

At work, I heard some colleagues talking about review courses they were taking to help them pass the CPA exam. I went home, did some research and found two review courses that had good ratings. One review course was strictly exam material based and the other review course was an in-person instructor led review course. I opted for the in-person instructor led course. I signed up immediately!

The review course I chose was five nights a week for 10 straight weeks. The first day I arrived, I noticed the class was filled with 35 students of which most were young white males. I was the only person of color in the room. I stuck out like a sore thumb. However, this didn't bother me because I was used to it at this point. Although this review course was not some magic wand that guaranteed us that we would pass the exam, it definitely helped. I came up with my own study plan. I studied one section at a time, reviewing the concepts, studying the guides, and answering practice exam questions. I followed this plan until I consistently scored a passing grade of 80%. I worked 8:00 am - 6:30 pm, grabbed a snack and raced to my review course from 7:00-9:00 pm. I spent many nights and most weekends in the library or at home studying. I was cooped up indoors, nose down with hopes to grind and shine. I was feeling good about my study plan, practice test scores and additional reference materials I gained from attending the review course.

When exam time came back around, I had a new confidence. I arrived early to give myself a chance to shake off the nerves. I entered the room with a positive mind, hoping that all the sacrifices I made would pay off. Armed with No. 2 pencils in my hand and a stack of scratch paper the proctor provided, I was ready. When the proctor signaled that we could begin, all I could hear was the sound of paper shuffling as everyone ripped open their exam. We were given four hours to complete this exam, but after only thirty minutes, several people got up, turned in the exams and left. It was mathematically impossible to answer all those questions in just thirty minutes. Clearly, they had given up on trying to pass the exam. As I took the exam, I made a point not to stay on any one question for more than two minutes. I did not want to run out of time for completing the exam. When I was unsure about the answer, I put a mark by the question to revisit that question later. I finished the exam within two and half hours. I revisited my answers to questions that I found to be particularly tricky. I only changed a few answers because the general test taking rule was to stick to your first answer. I scanned my hand prepared financial statements and did a final scan of my exam answers. When I turned in my exam, there were still many test takers still working. I was not the first to leave, but I finished with time to spare. I was exhausted when I turned in my exam and went home to take a nap. It was the month of April when I took the exam, and I would not learn the outcome until August.

Four months passed before I received my test scores in the mail. If your scores came in a long manila envelope, that meant that you passed zero to three parts of the four parts of the exam; it meant you did not pass all four parts. If your exam scores came in a white standard envelope from the Licensing Board of the State of Michigan, that meant that you passed all four parts. My exam results were sent in a long manila envelope. I tore open the envelope and to my surprise it was good news! I had passed three of the four parts which meant I only needed to pass one more part of the exam. I was thrilled and exhausted at the same time. I was happy I passed three parts, but I also wanted to be done. I took a break, celebrated, and went back to studying.

I had no idea that becoming a CPA was such a lofty goal. As I mentioned earlier, Marie Farell-Donalson was the first black woman CPA, certified in the state of Michigan. She accomplished that around 1973. That was only 12 years prior to my graduating from college. Passing the exam would put me on a noticeably short list of black female CPAs. Even today, Black CPAs (men and women combined) make up less than 1% (.76%) of all CPAs in the entire United States. Lofty goal or not, there was no turning back for me.

It was exam time again, but my circumstances were a bit different as my pregnancy had advanced. I waddled myself through the door and had a seat. The guy seated to my left was sweating profusely, so I struck up a conversation with him figuring it would help both of us to relax. The guy to my right was chewing on his fingernails and sipping water. As for me, I had prayed before coming to the exam because I needed to be done. I was feeling a little nervous and moderately confident.

August could not arrive soon enough. And when it did, I was searching the mailbox every day looking for an open-faced white envelope from the Licensing Board of the State of Michigan. One evening, I peered into my mailbox, and there it was! A white envelope with my name on it. Hands trembling, I ripped it open and straightened it out so I could read it.

The letter said, "Congratulations! Karen Hoskin, we are pleased to inform you that you have passed the Certified Public Accountant exam in the state of Michigan." I PASSED! YOUR GIRL PASSED THE CPA EXAM! On that day, August 19, 1988, I became a Certified Public Accountant (CPA)!

I had started out in corporate America in public accounting and it was rough to say the least, but I left with a skill and credentials that would open many doors in the future.

I learned valuables lessons there and I was thankful:

LESSON #1

Stay somewhere long enough to grow your skills and become an expert in your field. When I began in public accounting, I thought it was the worst decision. I ended up working with all types of people; some were friendly, but many were rude. Some were great colleagues, and many were prejudiced. But in the end, I was glad I continued to show up every morning.

Stay somewhere long enough to grow your skills and become an expert in your field.

LESSON # 2

Passing the CPA exam and becoming certified was something I did for ME. Also, this experience taught me that I had to manage my own career. I learned that nobody is going to manage your career for you. This entire experience was tough, but receiving my certification was rewarding.

Never to quit your job just because it's difficult. Sometimes you have to stay and boss up!

2
Being Let Go – Fired

No one wants to be walked out of a job with a white box. The shame and embarrassment of being dismissed from an assignment is an awful feeling. Four years into my career, I accepted a position as a senior accounting analyst at a mid-size service company, V-Xanaerro Corporation. As the senior accounting analyst, I would be responsible for looking at the financial statements and statements of cash flows. I nailed the interview and passed the senior accounting analyst exam and was ready to get started. I always wanted this type of job and was beyond excited about starting this position. I was hired by the CEO Dan and the finance director, Joe. Dan was witty, flamboyant, and easy going. He frequently wore designer business suits, with a shirt and tie. Joe was outspoken, analytical, and inquisitive. As the finance director, Joe was responsible for financial planning, forecasts, and budgets. The company had been in existence for ten years and Dan built it from the ground up. He had lots to boast about as it grew into a multi-million-dollar company.

It was a cold winter day as I headed toward my new office. I had my box of decorative goodies: a plant, plaques, and a coffee mug. I walked in with my big smile, greeting everyone along the path. I met my team, Shantell, Emma and Carol. We started to get to know each other as we shared stories and ate bagels. Before I knew it, the day had sped by and it was time to meet my predecessor, Linda. She had stopped by to give me a handoff of where things stood. Linda was every bit of the stereotypes of accountants shown on television. She was tall, lanky, fair-skinned and middle aged. She sported small, wire rimmed prescription glasses, her hair was pulled back in a bun and she looked like she was stressed. Trying to not notice her weariness, I invited her to have a seat so that we could get started. As Linda began to talk, it was kind of weird. It seemed as if she was there, but her mind was somewhere else. She indicated that everything was in good order except for the Company bank reconciliations. Per Linda, these bank reconciliations were a pain. Somehow, she had fallen behind on reconciling them. It sounded complicated, but I was too excited to care. As soon as she left, I dove into the bank reconciliations. There were numerous investments and monies flowing in and out of the company accounts and it was for sure a complicated mess. As I dug in, there was a knock at my office door. Emma entered, closed the door, and quickly took a seat. Emma was in her twenties, tall and slim. She came to tell me that she had already put in her two weeks' notice and she was leaving. 'Man!' I thought. This was my first day and already someone was quitting. Emma and I had hit it off well just a few hours earlier. We learned that we were both single parents and both our children had just begun pre-school. Emma said she had been planning to leave for quite some time now, and as people often do when they leave an organization, she had some information she wanted to share.

Emma said, "Be aware of Shantell, because she applied for your job and was angry that she did not get it." Next, she said she was leaving because she didn't like working with Joe. She said he was always asking her to process checks but he frequently was late with providing the invoices. She said his workflow was chaotic and as the accounts payable clerk, that made her job harder. Then she had a big secret she wanted me to know. The secret was that Joe was Dan's cousin. Nobody knew this information except the "insiders" that Dan and Joe considered to be family. She was tired of all the inconsistencies in the expectations of her on the job. I thanked her for sharing and expressed my disappointment that she was leaving.

Meeting with Joe was Impossible

I started to formalize my first impression of Joe who was my boss. My first impression of him was that he barked out orders to colleagues. Some colleagues seem to like him, but others seemed annoyed by him. He had the reputation of making money for the Company so even the seemingly annoyed colleagues followed his guidance. I wanted to meet with Joe, but he was constantly in meetings. Getting face time with him seemed impossible. He said I had his full support but at the same time, he was not making himself available. I wanted to share with him my intent to implement some standard procedures for how we conducted our business. Perhaps I was moving too fast on this. It's been recommended by business savvy folks that it is best not to make too many changes in your first 90 to 100 days on a job. While considering this, I elected instead to get ready for our auditors who were coming to town.

Our auditors rolled in bright and early on a Monday morning and I was ready for them. As a former auditor, I knew what they were looking for and why. Concerned about the state of the bank reconciliations, I decided to bring this to their attention immediately. These bank reconciliations were a mess and were not reconcilable. I had inherited this mess and there were just too many missing pieces to work backwards to get them reconciled. The auditors agreed and suggested that I write off the total irreconcilable balance to start with a clean slate. I agreed with their assessment but hated to right off such a large balance. I assured them that such discrepancies would not happen on my watch.

After the auditors left, I was finally going to get some face time with Joe. When I met with him, Dan also tagged along. Joe started off the conversation, "I don't think you are the right person for this job." For about twenty seconds my mind went blank. I felt like someone slapped me into a nightmare. What did he mean by saying that I was not the right person for this job? If I wasn't the right person for the job, who was? We had a clean audit except for the messy bank reconciliations I had inherited, and I was just approaching 90 days on the job. Not to mention, he had not made any time to meet prior to now. I had come to this job as a qualified CPA and had passed the senior accounting analyst exam administered by an outside firm. Yes, I was brand new to the role, but my gosh, I had not been on the job 90 days and had not been given the chance to prove myself. Dan on the other hand, sat quietly, then turned to me and said, "Would you be willing to take the staff accountant analyst role?"

While feeling like I had been cut with a razor, I told Dan I would take the staff accountant analyst role. Joe appeared shocked and angry, but why? I would later learn that Dan rarely questioned Joe's decisions on anything. I was collecting my emotions, but I was hurt. When the workday ended, I stopped by my dad's house to share this news. My dad was typically happy and high spirited but as I shared what happened, wrinkles began forming in his forehead. Dad was angry. He said, "They demoted you." Dad was expressing his disapproval and I did not get the sense that he thought I should have agreed to take that lower position. However, he respected my decision.

The next several months at work looked like a circus as I watched one senior accounting analyst after another grace our doors and eventually leave. The average tenure for these folks was about three weeks. As the staff accounting analyst, I kept all my pre-existing job duties, so I wasn't sure what the new senior accounting analyst's responsibilities were. One of those senior accounting analyst candidate's names was Nick. Nick was pale with blue eyes and blonde hair, medium built and short. He was friendly and greeted everyone with "Top of the morning." He looked like a happy, confident fellow, but the truth was, Nick did not know what to do but he would not ask for any help. And just like with me, Joe did not give him the time of the day. It seemed like Joe didn't care what Nick did just as long as he stayed out of his hair. I was starting to see a pattern; Joe did not collaborate or establish a rapport with any analysts. As the senior accounting analyst candidates came and went, I wondered if in the meantime, Joe would finally notice and admit that I was doing a great job.

One day while looking through our records, I noticed a large payment that looked odd. I asked the team for documentation, but they suggested that I ask Joe. When I stopped in Joe's office, he did not seem to recall the details but assured me that he would investigate it. Having a bad feeling about it, I wanted to dig further, but Joe peered up from his computer and dismissed it. A few days later, I came across another odd-looking item. It was a large check that had been signed by Joe, made out to some random vendor. Joe had check signing authority and had not been accountable to anyone. I asked him details about the check, but he just smiled and said, "You're over analyzing." Once again, I had a bad feeling about it just like I did about the prior transaction. Here we had two large transactions with little to no supporting documentation nor explanations. As I thought about these things, I began to realize what was going on. I had a horrible gut feeling that Joe and possibly someone else with him was stealing money. Some things were making sense now. First, Joe never wanted me to put policies in place that would hold people accountable, including himself. Joe had been notorious for not providing documentation for checks he signed. Secondly, he never took time off, except on company holidays. People who steal often do not take days off to protect their theft from being discovered. He and Emma had bumped heads many times because he had her make checks payable to companies and individuals without invoices or other supporting documentation. Then there were the discombobulated bank reconciliations, and now that the bank reconciliations were perfectly balanced, he more than likely wanted to restore them to a state of chaos in order to steal. But how was I going to tell Dan all of this? Joe was Dan's cousin. I needed tangible, concrete evidence before I could go to Dan accusing him.

More time had flown by and I still did not have the proof I needed. Going to work had become uneasy. I was sitting in my office when Joe stepped in. 'This was a nice change,' I thought. But, he entered in like a mailman dropping off a package. He gave me an envelope and told me today was my last day and that I was fired. If there was an award to be given for an element of surprise, Joe would win it hands down. Why was I still surprised? I had removed much of the chaos in the workplace that he had created. Our books and records were too clean and too auditable for him, so I had to go. As Joe left, I closed my office door and started packing the dreaded "you are fired, white box." My heart was broken. A few minutes later, David knocked on the door. He was a wonderful colleague and supporter. He had been excited for me getting this role. When he saw me packing my personal belongings, he looked on in silence. I said, "Well, David, this is my last day." His eyes began to swell up and he cried. I was thinking in my head, wow he is crying real tears. It was nice to know someone cared about me. With his help, it only took me one trip to the car. Thankfully, no one saw me walking out with my white box. As I pulled away from the property, the tears rolled down my cheeks and I sobbed loudly. When I got home, I opened the envelope and found a lump sum check. This check could pay some bills for a bit. I wanted to be practical with this money, but I could only think of one thing.

The best thing in my life was my daughter. I had enrolled her in a Christian school that was in great demand because of their academic excellence. I was fortunate to get a spot for my daughter after being on the waiting list for months. Now that I was fired, how could I afford to keep her in private school? What was going to happen to her dreams? I could not bear the thought of her being separated from her friends or losing the quality education she was receiving. So, the very next day, I went to her school and paid her tuition for the remainder of the school year with most of the lump sum. I did not do the practical thing, but I told myself that somehow, we would be alright.

Months went by and the reality of the economy sunk in. I was fired during a time when jobs were scarce. I started running out of money. I still had to pay the mortgage and car note. I didn't have much savings, so I started looking for which expenses I could cut. The gas bill skyrocketed as I fell way behind on paying it. They shut off the gas and I began heating our house with the electric stove. I did that for a while but then a pipe burst in the kitchen. Finally, I called my dad, and explained my financial situation. I asked him if we could live with him until I could get back on my feet. I had been searching and searching for work.

I eventually got a job as a substitute teacher. The pay sounded like it would be fair, and I was grateful to be working. The school where I was assigned was a multi-cultural school and I loved that. I became the resident substitute math teacher while the primary math teacher was out on maternity leave. I liked substitute teaching and I liked the kids.

It was Friday and I was looking forward to the weekend. I raced across town to pick up my daughter from school. When we got home, I had mail. It was my first paycheck. I opened the envelope with confident expectation and looked at the check. When I saw the paycheck amount, I was floored. This was not the amount of money I was expecting - it was much less. For a moment, I was wondering if it was an error. But after some phone calls, I found out the pay was correct. My next thought was "I have got to get back to my profession." I spent the next weeks praying, asking God for direction, and looking for places to apply.

I called my former colleague Harris. He was still working at a prior employer I had left before joining V-Xanaerro Corporation. However, Harris was no longer working in the department we had both worked in. With his advice, I reached out to a mutual colleague that was in the department I left and asked her to give my resume to her director. With

God's grace, I was hired and started my new job right after winter break. Although I was grateful for the substitute teaching opportunity, I was more grateful to be working back in the field of accounting. As a parent, I needed to be able to properly take care of my daughter. This had been a tough season. In time, I was able to get my finances back on track and we returned to our own home. Life was restored, there was harmony and I ended up staying at that company for four years.

The sound of television in the living room was background entertainment while I was cooking dinner. All of a sudden, the phone rang. When I answered the phone, I did recognize the voice at first. Then the caller spoke my nickname. He said, "Kay Kay, it's me David from V-Xanaerro Corporation." It had been at least three years since I last saw David. We bumped into each other at an education seminar at the time. He said, "I wanted to share with you what just happened at V-Xanaerro Corporation. The government performed an investigation of the financial records of V-Xanaerro. Joe and two other employees at V-Xanaerro have been indicted for embezzlement and handed over to the authorities. Dan has been talking to the media about it." The truth had finally come out for all the world to see. I was wrongfully fired, but with the truth being out, I felt vindicated.

In your career, there are going to be lessons, triumphs, and disappointments, but you will persevere! In every seemingly bad experience, there is something good in it.

In your career, there are going to be lessons, triumphs, and disappointments, but you will persevere!

3
Horrible Bosses

Sometimes you may have a wonderful job, but a horrible boss(es). It is not always wise to just up and leave when you have a horrible boss. You have to make sure you're getting what you need out of each work experience. We often have to get our feet wet, stay long enough and get some work experience under our belt. So, we have to figure out how to deal with these leaders. Many times, they may not be bad people, but they have issues.

It can be hard being managed by bosses you do not like or do not respect. You may even want to help them but they may not be open to feedback. But, there are many lessons we can learn from bad bosses, including what not to do when leading people. I had to learn to dig deep to flow with these managers and to respect their authority, regardless of my likes or dislikes for them. So, this chapter is dedicated to all of my bad bosses. It was from these experiences that I learned how to keep my cool and maintain my professionalism.

The Disruptive Micro Manager

My second job after college was with a major health care provider.

Business was booming, so they hired 12 of us to be hospital reimbursement professionals. I, as usual, was excited to get started! I loved new job opportunities. But this work experience would not play out the way I thought. I would soon learn what it meant to be micromanaged. The most annoying thing about micro managers is that they think they are adding value, efficiency and productivity. But what actually ends up happening is that they hinder the team's performance from all of their hand holding, baby-sitting and disruptions. What you want is to be a professional who is trusted to do your job, but this type of manager is more interested in controlling what happens, when it happens and how it happens.

We each were assigned to a senior leader for whom we would report. My leader was Brandy, a middle-aged lady with a southern accent. She would arrive at our office at 7:00 am so that she could give me detailed instructions of what she wanted completed, what order she wanted it completed in and how she wanted it to be completed. When I arrived at the office, Brandy had a detailed written note in my chair, a long email that she sent me and a voicemail that she left me. Then, the moment I arrived and sat in my chair, she was standing behind me to verbally tell me everything she had already said on the written note, personal email and voicemail left.

So, every day our workday went like this: 1) take the handwritten work assignments out of our chairs, read the assignments 2) read the detailed email work instructions she sent 3) proceed to play back her voicemail of those work assignments and 4) expect her to be standing behind you, the moment you first arrive. Her voicemails went something like this: "Hello Karen. This is Brandy. I want you to start working on the assignments I left at your desk. Please read everything. I want you to perform the review of XYZ and so on and more. I want you to number the workpapers in sequence A-1.1, A-1.2 and so on. Then I want you to perform a review of the leasing documents for ABC hospital. Number those workpapers C-1.1, C-1.2 and so on. Okay, talk to you later. Bye." When she visited our cubes, she repeated everything that she already said to us earlier, in her handwritten assignments, work emails and voicemails. This drove me nuts! and that is why I named her **the disruptive micro manager**. She never left us alone to do our jobs, instead, she was overseeing our every move and constantly being disruptive every day!

I felt like I was in the movie Office Space. Office Space is a hilarious comedy about a group of employees fed up with their mind-numbing workplace. In one scene, one of the employees, Peter Gibbons, forgets to put the cover sheet on his "T.P.S report." Boss number #1 stops by and says, "Hey Peter, did you get the memo that we're putting cover sheets on all of our T.P.S reports?"

Peter says, "Yes I got the memo, I just forgot this one time."

Then, boss #2 comes to Peter's desk and says, "Did you get the memo that we're putting cover sheets on all of our T.P.S reports? I will resend you the memo."

Peter tries to explain, but Boss #2 cuts him off and says, "Be sure to use the cover sheet on your "T.P.S reports. Thanks."

Then, Peter's phone rings. He listens, then answers with "Yes, I got the memo about the "T.P.S reports." The first time I saw this, I cried laughing! I could relate so much. Peter had several bosses reminding him of the same thing. Brandy could have been one of the bosses in Office Space. She managed to give us the same instructions at least four times every day. She was the supervisor that got on everybody's nerves. One of the ways we learned to deal with her was to laugh about her micromanager ways.

At some point in our work assignments, it required us to make visits to the hospitals and work offsite. Brandy showed up at our work offsites to watch what we were doing and to disrupt our day with her presence. But we soon learned that Brandy also had a hidden agenda. While she was working overtime to keep us working, Brandy was also getting her hair done during work hours. The days that we worked offsite were the days Brandy was getting her hair done and arrived at our locations directly after her hair appointments. So, Brandy was not only a **disruptive micromanager**, but she was also an irresponsible person who lacked character and integrity.

Mr. Houdini

There are some people who just excel in influencing people. They are charming and charismatic. They excel in the "soft" skills and emotional intelligence. I had a boss like this. His name was Ethan. He could calm and diffuse every situation. He knew how to make each person feel valued. Ethan was smart, friendly, and outgoing. He was equally liked by both the women and the men. He was charismatic, and it was because of these things, Ethan had been promoted to manager. But something bad happened over the years after his promotion. Ethan changed. He went from being a dependable, responsible manager to an undependable and elusive slacker. During work hours, many people would be looking for him, and by early afternoon, no one knew his whereabouts. We often could not find him to address questions that needed managerial attention. It wasn't long before his absence became the talk of the office. The almost daily question on the floor was, "Where is Ethan?" Someone eventually nicknamed Ethan after Harry Houdini who was famous for illusions and escape artistry. Ethan was our very own **Mr. Houdini**.

There was one weekend that everyone on Ethan's team had to work on Saturday due to a deadline that none of us were told about. We all arrived at the office early on Saturday morning. Everyone was present but Ethan, and team members were pretty grumpy because it was a beautiful summer day in Michigan but we were all cooped up in the office, working with our nose to the grind. Ethan's work was being completed by our supervisor in his absence. We were finishing up the work when all of a sudden Ethan walked in. He was dressed in his finest golfing apparel. He flashed his pearly smile, thanked everybody for coming in and left. We later learned that one of the reasons Ethan came up missing so much was because he was leaving our office during work hours to work on a new franchise. Ethan who was once a likeable, dependable manager was now just a scammer, stealing tons of hours from his current job to work on his personal endeavors. Now, it's okay to break up your work day if you have flexible working arrangements, but to consistently do your own thing during work hours is not okay.

The Life Jacket Boss

I experienced several years of success in my career with a particular company, but changes were taking place in the company that made all but a few of us want to jump ship. They were moving the headquarters to Texas. We did not know if our jobs were going to be moved there too. I felt uneasy about all of this, so I made a phone call to a corporate recruiter and landed an interview with a prominent company. To prepare, I did all the things you need to do when preparing for an interview. I tailored my resume to align with the job posting. I researched the company, mapped out questions and prepared my interview strategy. That following Monday, I went to the interview. This interview was conducted panel style. It was a grueling three and half hours, but all my preparation paid off. I got the job! Not only did I get the job, but I also landed a substantial pay increase. Back then, I thought more money was an answer for happiness and joy in the workplace. I could not have been more wrong. You and I are responsible for our own happiness, not a job, not a person, not anything.

> *You and I are responsible for our own happiness, not a job, not a person, not anything.*

The job I left had a wonderful culture. My colleagues and I were close, like family. I was hoping for a similar experience in this new role.

I began my new job in July and my birthday was later in the month. I had met my manager during the interview. Her name was Susan. When I arrived at the office, she took me around and introduced me to the team. The entire staff of women and men were of varying ages, but none of them looked like me. I had experienced this my whole career. But I was more interested in their character than their color. So, I was ready to get this experience going.

Most of my colleagues did not like Susan. The word on the floor was that Susan was not performing her job well. It seems like some people get to keep their jobs for reasons that have nothing to do with work performance. It also seems like no matter what they do wrong, they do not get fired. Susan, I was told, was one of those people. My colleagues said Susan was a backstabber who never took responsibility for her failures. The senior manager tried to find a spot for her somewhere else in the company but was unsuccessful. He would not fire her though. That would reflect poorly on him because he hired her. I was too new to know if their claims were true, but when a manager is not fired no matter how incompetent you think they are, these managers have protection. They are **bosses with life jackets, a.k.a. Life Jacket Bosses**; That means no matter what they do, these bosses will never be fired and will never lose their paychecks.

I met with Susan to discuss my work plan. I mapped out due dates and a schedule and I began work on my first assignment. Our finished work product is always put into a report. I was able to finish the assignment early and put everything into a report. I turned the report into Susan for her to review it and provide feedback. The protocol was: I submitted my reports to Susan, Susan reviewed the reports I gave her, and she provided feedback. Once Susan provided me feedback, I answered her review comments and returned the reports to her. It was then Susan's job to pass the reports to our senior manager, so that he could review them and sign-off. I emailed my report to Susan. Her reply was that she would take a look at it and get back to me. Another two weeks went by and I still did not have any feedback from her. I casually stopped by her desk to check in. Susan spoke with a lisp. I asked if she had a chance to look at my report and her reply was "Okay, I will take a look at it and get back to you." This happened three more times with three more reports. I would send the reports to Susan for her review, but she was always late in turnaround of her reviews. I started getting frustrated, because I was submitting my reports on time, but she was consistently late in reviewing them. Then I found out that Susan was telling our senior manager that she was waiting for me to submit my reports. I was angry now, but my colleagues had warned me. They had even said Mike on our team had been passed over for promotion because he was "burned" by Susan. The truth was Susan showed up for work every day, but she was constantly missing reporting deadlines, and when she fell behind, she blamed her staff. It was my turn to see this side of her. I was the new girl, and she was making me her fall guy. A few more days went by and sure enough, our senior manager sent an email to me and Susan asking where the reports were.

I responded, "I sent those reports to Susan "x" number of days ago."

After my response, Susan stopped by my desk. She was breathing hard while simultaneously trying to mask her anger. I had embarrassed her and she was determined to make me pay for it. She began to question my work, and now I had to defend everything I submitted to her. I really did not realize how bad things were. Susan became picky about all of my work and the conclusions I wrote in the reports. She made it seem like everything I did was wrong. She questioned my understanding of my role and suggested that I get a mentor. The next thing I knew, I was on a performance plan. Now I was required to meet with her and HR weekly. I thought, 'are you kidding me?' I felt like I had to defend myself. I started documenting my version of things and bringing it to these HR meetings, and now I had even more work to do because I had all these extra assignments from HR. I had to seek other manager's feedback on my work. I had to look for a mentor. Susan was not going to let me enjoy not one day. I went out to lunch one day with some friends, Susan called me at lunchtime. I rarely left the building because we had a cafeteria, but on this one day, I met friends for lunch, she called. Who does that?

I was in the midst of an uphill battle when I met an employee named Kathy. She was a very friendly, upbeat person who smiled a lot and shared great stories. I met her while requesting certain documents from her department. During a conversation, I found out Kathy was a Christian like me, and we attended the same church. Our church was very large so meeting people we later learned attended our church was not uncommon. We decided to meet for lunch in the cafeteria. We became friends and began having lunch together on a regular basis. One day, I opened up to Kathy about my work situation. I told her about my weekly meetings with Susan and HR. Kathy looked concerned. She said, "What is your manager saying in these meetings?"

This was an eye-opening question. I was so focused on defending my work, I wasn't really listening to what Susan was saying.

The next time I went to the weekly meeting with Susan and HR, I asked Susan how she felt I was progressing. I shared Susan's feedback with Kathy. Kathy helped me to realize that Susan did not just have me on a performance plan but was planning to fire me. I was shocked. I had never been on a performance plan and did not know what to expect. I was not expecting to be fired. Prior to Kathy's counsel, I was fighting back, or so I thought. I was writing my viewpoints and trying to counter Susan's. I wrote a whole story that I gave to HR. But sadly, I came to realize, HR was not on my side; they rarely are in these types of situations. Susan had the "keys to the car," so to speak, and she was driving. Kathy helped me to see that I needed to change my attitude, even though this situation was unfair and painful. I needed to stop trying to defend myself. My bad attitude had made things worse. For the remaining weeks of the performance plan, I returned to my cheerful self and I was kind. But Susan's plan was to fire me. By the time I connected all the dots, it was too late. Susan succeeded in getting me fired. My colleagues were right; no one at the job held her accountable for her strained relationships with colleagues nor for her poor work performance. She was indeed a boss with a life jacket. **And the Life Jacket Bosses never get fired.**

Lessons learned

No matter how much you think or know your boss is incompetent or unfair, you must respect their role. Respect them, all the way up to the time you walk out the door, and do not burn bridges. You never know who knows who out here. Susan was a bad boss, but I did not manage our relationship or myself properly. It does not mean that Susan was right in firing me and it does not mean that it was fair. This turned out to be a character growth opportunity for me. Character growths are a necessary part of life and your journey.

Maybe you have been let go from a job for one reason or another. Your career is not over if you've been let go from a job no matter the circumstance. You are created to do some awesome things in this life. Do not let this event discourage you. You will rise again! Dust that experience off, learn from it, and move on. When you have a moment to process things, truthfully ask yourself, why did they let me go? Was it just an economic downturn? Do you see an opportunity to correct some things within you? Was it just not a good fit? Did you have good relationships in that work environment? Did you and your manager clash? Did you clash with colleagues?

Now, the fact that you do not like your manager can be real. However, that may not mean it's time to leave the position. In your career, there are risks. Write down why you want to move on. Pray about it, talk to mentors, select friends and family you trust to talk about it and to help you make the right decision.

Before you leave a position, train your replacement. If appropriate, for example, when you take a role within the same company, make yourself available for pockets of time to help them with the transition of your former duties.

Remember, no bad situation lasts forever, get up and get at it again. When things like this happen, assess what you could have done differently or will do differently in the future. Sometimes you look at what others did wrong and it serves as a wake-up call not to engage in that type of behavior. Take those lessons into the next opportunity. Do not hold grudges, even if you feel like they did you wrong. Just let it go! Your health, prosperity and peace of mind are more important than a difficult work experience. In all things, there is always something positive you can gain from any situation, but you must look for it. One positive thing I learned from this experience is to "manage upward".

Managing upwards is being able to manage your relationship with your boss + his/her expectations + his/her perception of your performance.

When I say, "manage upward" I am saying that your relationship with your direct manager needs to be a good relationship. I don't care how incompetent you think he or she is, you must effectively manage that relationship and respect their position of authority. At the end of the day, it is great if you like your manager, but if you do not, you still need to respect their authority.

When these lessons come, acknowledge where you may have missed it, forgive yourself and forgive the people involved. It may take a while, but you can forgive them. Take hold of the lessons, but release the pain. It is possible that you were in the wrong work assignment to begin with. As the late Chadwick Boseman said, "Sometimes you need to feel the pain and sting of defeat to activate the real passion and purpose that

God predestined inside of you."

> *"Sometimes you need to feel the pain and sting of defeat to activate the real passion and purpose that God predestined inside of you."* - CHADWICK BOSEMAN

Fast forward, several years after I was fired, I bumped into Susan who had put me on a performance plan and had succeeded in getting me fired. We bumped into each other at a courtesy conference given by our mutual service provider. Susan was shocked to see me and that I was doing well, so polished, favored and highly respected. That felt good and when I saw Susan I was not angry. I was not resentful. I was poised, professional and confident.

Bumping into Susan was a reminder to never burn bridges because you don't know when you will meet up with these people again or who knows who. I was also reminded of how I had grown in dealing with difficult people including difficult bosses. The version of myself that bumped into Susan was more disciplined emotionally and much smarter about dealing with people in authority. I learned to always look at bosses' position of authority and to respect that position. I realize that life is all about how we manage our relationships and when we master our relationships at work, work life is better.

4
The Unemployment Season

Getting fired never feels good and often there is a feeling of remorse. We tend to equate being fired with failure, but most of the time there are other reasons why the firing occurred. Sometimes you're fired because you're in the wrong assignment. Sometimes you're fired because the role you were in was holding you back from something better. Sometimes you're fired because you lack wisdom. It still hurts though, but it doesn't last forever.

Once I was fired from the job with Susan, I was unemployed for a while. This firing occurred during the recession of 2007/2008. When money got scarce, I got creative and reinvented myself as a consultant, a.k.a. contractor. I went from being a full-time employee to someone who was hired out to companies for certain periods of time, usually to assist with projects. I received my work assignments through consulting firms aka contracting houses. They called me when a company had a need in my area of knowledge. The blessing in working for contracting houses was that I got to see a variety of work processes, worked for different companies and had the opportunity to provide diverse solutions. The work that came through the contracting houses was not consistent though and I began to think of what other ways I could possibly make some money.

A Decision to Create Another Stream of Income

While contemplating how I could increase my financial position, I got a bright idea that I should flip houses. If I am honest, this decision I made to flip houses did not feel right, but I told myself this was going to help me financially. So, I went into business with Randy, an acquaintance, who seemed to have done well in flipping houses. I had good credit, so I used my good credit to buy a Detroit property to flip. Randy had successfully flipped several houses, so he and I made a deal. The deal was that we would fix the house up, get it up to city code. That was doable and we agreed to what percent we would split from the proceeds of flipping the house. But in the middle of everything, Randy left town and I was stuck with a property I did not know how to sell. I went from being excited to being scared. I did not know what to do, so I called Charles; he was one of Randy's contractors. I hired Charles to fix up the property to get it ready for sale. I bought materials, appliances, fixtures, all the works. I also bought aluminum siding to repair the garage. I ended up racking up a lot of credit card debt, but in my mind, I was certain that I was about to get paid.

Months started going by, but Charles had not completed much work. He did some of the work, but then said he needed to hire other contractors to help. He made excuses and insisted that he was lining up a buyer. I lived on the other side of town. As time went on, I stopped going to the property. Then one morning, Charles called me in distress. He said, "Karen, the property has been broken into and everything is GONE." My heart dropped in disbelief! I met him at the property to see what had happened. Everything was indeed gone and I was distraught! In hindsight, I am convinced that Charles stole everything or had an accomplice. After the break in, I was afraid and did not go check on the property anymore.

Finally, one day I decided to go check on the property. I didn't want to go by myself, so I called my sister. I needed backup in case I ran into an unwelcoming situation. You know how you call that one person who has your back if something jumps off wrong? My sister "came with." We jumped in the car and headed to my property. I knocked on the door before I turned my key. As I turned the key, I heard a voice. The person on the other side of the door began to unlock the door. My mind was racing and I was thinking, 'Oh my God! Who is this person?' When the door opened, it was a young woman, a man and a couple of teenagers. Come to find out Charles had moved a family into MY property and was collecting rent! The nerve of this guy! Now I not only had a property that I had not been able to sell, but I also had "squatters." Of course, when I contacted Charles, he pretended to not know these people and denied collecting rent from them. However, I had a lengthy conversation with the woman who answered the door and I asked her to describe her landlord. Based on her description, it was Charles all right. He just gave her a phony name. My so-called business partner, Charles may have not only robbed me but also secretly moved a family into my property. This was too much! Could this property situation get any worse?

I finally did what I should have done in the first place. I prayed about what I should do. I concluded that I should reach out to Lucas. Lucas was a potential buyer that was interested in the property early on. This was before I spent a ton of money trying to get the property up to code. My goal had been to get this property up to code, sell it and make a sizable profit. But instead, I ended up selling that property to Lucas for a little of nothing.

Consultant Workflow

A brighter side of things began to happen as the work calls came in. Being a contractor can be demanding. You cannot be timid or fearful. You must quickly add value to that organization. The contractor's life is not like an employee. The company who contracts for your services can let you go at any time. If you don't add value, you're out. On the other hand, when you are a consultant or contractor, you get many more opportunities to grow your skills and experiences.

There were some great things that came out of this unemployment season. First, I developed thicker skin. Second, I got lots of opportunities to work for different companies. By the time I went back to full time employment, I had far more experience, knowledge, and skill than my counterparts. There were also other good things that came out of the unemployment season. As a contractor, I had pockets of time where I was not working. When a contract ended, I had weeks of open time off.

The greatest benefit of the unemployment season was the extra time I had to spend with my daughter, Jill. Jill was attending Wayne State, commuting back and forth from school to home. When Jill came home, I would have lunch ready. She would share the details of her day. We watched reruns of the Gilmore Girls. Gilmore girls is the story of a small town centered around Lorelai Gilmore, a flamboyant single mom from an affluent family and her daughter Rory. Their characters reminded us of our own relationship, and like Jill and I, the mom and daughter were close. Jill and I would come up with creative ways to have fun without spending a ton of money. We would create exploration trips and visit quaint shops in the neighborhood. These times Jill and I had together were some of the most memorable times of our lives. Finances were tight but I would not have traded that time with Jill for anything else.

When I recovered from this unemployed season, I put some financial practices in place.

When I recovered from this season, I put in some financial practices in place. And the first thing I did was stash cash.

Here are some practical things to do to recover financially:
- *Stash cash - You need a 6 to 9-month emergency fund of salary.*
- *Make a budget – start weekly, then by pay period. Use Excel or*

an app. Look for things to cut out. E.g., Do your own hair and polish your own nails. Stop paying for stuff you do not use e.g., gym memberships, deluxe cable

- *Pay yourself every pay period – every pay period put money into your emergency fund. No exceptions. Do it. No matter how small.*
- *Reinvent yourself, but do not ruin your current gig if employed*
- *Pay your bills – pay your rent and proceed from there*
  - *Do not hide from your creditors. Call your creditors – make payment arrangements*
  - *Negotiate your payments. Many of them will accept small payments.*
- *Live below your means – e.g., move to a cheaper place to live*
- *Reduce your expenses e.g., cook vs. eating out, stop reckless shopping*
- *Treat yourself – once a pay period; buy something inexpensive that you like*
- *Sell some stuff – what do you have in your house? e.g., sell clothes on eBay.*
- *Do not spend student loan money like it is free – they will come for you.*
- *Research loan forgiveness and talk to your friends. In the meantime, pay it.*
- *Cut up credit cards or put them away.*

Listen to me. Your Auntie is speaking. Create a budget and save money. Keep an emergency fund of 6 to 9 months of your salary, and do not co-mingle that emergency fund money with bill money. You can open a free savings account at banks like Huntington.

Here are some high interest online savings accounts:
- *American Express Bank*

- *Capital One Bank*

- *Marcus by Goldman Sachs Bank*

Even when you are doing well financially, maintain a budget. If you don't manage your money, it will leave you. Channel your money, earn, budget, and invest. Keep a check on it and always have funds stored up for when economically challenging seasons come. The world's economy and our country's economy always go through peaks and lows, so be sure to plan so that you are always prepared when it happens.

5

25 Keys for How Not to Get Fired

I was talking with a friend about my book and he said he could have used this book a few years ago because he kept getting fired. My younger self also needed this book early on in my career. I needed a cheat sheet that I could follow to help me not make so many mistakes in the workforce. As a younger employee, I had a lot of opinions and I made a lot of mistakes. This list is intended to help you save some bumps on the head and to enrich your work-life experiences.

1. **Don't speak everything you're thinking.**
   This is common sense but some of us think that we can say any and everything we want to at work and it's just not true. The communication that comes out of your mouth should be respectful, meaningful, and not contentious. As the bible proverb says, "be quick to listen and slow to speak."

2. **Be kind; show empathy and care about others at work.**
   "What goes around, comes around." Some people call it karma. When people perceive you are a mean person or troublemaker,

you put yourself in position to learn less, earn less, have fewer opportunities, and potentially be alienated.

3. **Pray about the jobs you take and don't just take the ones that offer the highest pay.**
When you are in the wrong job, no amount of money will make you happy or make things right for you.

4. **Respect your boss and others even if you don't like them.** This is so important! As we've discussed earlier, a poor relationship with your supervisor can put you out of a job quickly. Respect your boss's position. Treat them the way they want to be treated. Do your job with integrity. Act your wage. Do what you're asked and paid to do. It can be hard, but do not say unflattering things about your boss, especially not at work. "Walls have ears." Instead, pray for your boss.

5. **Don't put your boss on blast in front of others.**

6. **Build a trusted relationship with your boss.**

7. **Don't put your co-workers on blast, especially not in front of their bosses or leaders.**

8. **Don't have a bad attitude. Your attitude does impact your aptitude.**

9. **Be diligent. Don't just do what's required, go over and beyond. Be excellent.**

10. **Know yourself. But be "you" in a respectful manner.** We all have character flaws that can ruin relationships at home and at work. Work on your character flaws. Be willing to apologize. Seek counseling if you need to.

11. **Don't challenge your boss' authority.**

12. **Don't be argumentative.**

13. **Be trustworthy. Don't lie, gossip nor defame people.**

14. **Stay away from envy, jealousy, and pride.**

15. **Do not steal time from your job.** They are paying you to do a job. If you are angry about something, manage your anger. You can pray, meditate, exercise or seek counseling.

16. **Be a good listener.**

17. **Lift others, cooperate and be a good team player.**

18. **Listen for advice, direction, and correction.** If valid, make the necessary adjustments.

19. **Seek mentors and feedback that will help you grow.**

20. **Don't be idle, instead learn a skill, take on a project, volunteer to help others.**

21. **Purpose not to bump heads.** Learn how to get along with others, but have the crucial conversations. Don't be petty.

22. **Manage your expectations. Be happy. Be patient.**

23. **Don't be a glory grabber.** Don't be that person who looks for ways to take credit for someone else's work.

24. **Don't over exaggerate your skillset in an interview.**

25. **Choose not to be disgruntled**. Find a way to work out your frustrations so that you can move up, move on and win.

Everyone makes mistakes, but if you listen to (me) your corporate auntie K, you can bypass a lot of them.

6
I Hate My Job

If you have worked in corporate America long enough, you have experienced this reality. You wake up, drag yourself out of bed, wait until the last minute to get dressed and if you live in Michigan during the winter you pray for a snow day. You drive to work slowly, stopping at all the lights and you walk in the door dreaming of your lunch break. Why? Because you hate your job. Most people hate their job for one of four reasons:

1. You hate the work you're doing.
2. You don't like the culture.
3. You don't like your boss or your co-workers.
4. You don't see any potential for upward mobility.

When I think about hating my job, a certain place comes to mind. The commute was painful, the pay was mediocre, the actual work was underwhelming, but above everything, my boss made me want to quit daily. I was just coming off of a two-year contracting gig and this was one of my first full time positions in a while. I was happy when I first got the job because the culture seemed lively and everyone was warm and welcoming. It wasn't until a couple of weeks in that I realized I was in for a rough road.

My supervisor was an introverted guy who spent most of his day staring at his computer screen and chatting with the boy's club in the office. And the only other time he spoke was when he was barking orders at his team. It was no secret that when month end reporting came around, our supervisor was completely stressed. On this particular day, I wasn't in the mood.

"You need to review these accounts by Monday! And I don't care about who has a problem with it! And get that reconciliation done now!" he barked.

As the yelling continued, I left mid-sentence and went to the cafeteria to cool off. When I returned, he was back at his computer, sitting down quietly as if nothing had happened. I had had enough. So at lunch time, I began to develop an exit plan.

This was my plan:
1. I would stay at this job for a year max. Recruiters and employers frown on candidates leaving a job in less than a year.
2. I would learn as much as I could about my current role and the industry to leverage it for my next job.
3. I would stay in touch with colleagues in my network and discuss potential opportunities.
4. I would build relationships with other leaders within the company because you never know where your next opportunity could come from.
5. I would stay in touch with recruiters and call them around the ninth month of being employed with the company.
6. I would volunteer to assist on at least one project outside of my role to build my resume.
7. I would work to exceed the agreed upon expectations discussed with my supervisor.

8. I would be sure not to burn bridges when I leave and stay professional in my communication.

If you know that you are unhappy at your current job and leaving is inevitable, always have a plan. Make sure you stay at least a year in the role. Even if your job is "hell" on earth, don't quit without having another offer in place. If you are a fan of the company, but not enjoying the culture in your department or not liking the work, maybe consider moving to a department within the company that has a culture more aligned with your core values. This is why it is important to maintain professionalism even when dealing with a difficult boss or coworker. This is easier said than done, but it is necessary to protect your personal brand. Your reputation will proceed you.

Here are a few more tips to help you transition out of the job you hate into a new opportunity:

1. Make friends with colleagues in other departments.
2. Find a support system of leaders and colleagues that want to see you succeed.
3. Don't rush into a new role before you have gotten everything you can out of your current work assignment.

Remember, you are responsible for your career. Have conversations with your supervisors throughout your career about your personal career goals. Also, look for opportunities to get involved with business resource groups within your company. Think about the social issues you are passionate about and get involved with a group that matches your core values. This will allow you to grow in leadership, give back, get to know other leaders and expand your network. Be patient, it takes a while to find your sweet spot in your career.

7
Negotiating Salaries

Men have no problem negotiating for salaries. It almost seems like (though not true) that it is a part of their DNA to do so. Men are taught at an early age to ask for what they want. They negotiate wages and nobody questions them about it. Women, on the other hand, have not been taught to negotiate wages. This creates a disparity in salaries between what men get paid and what women get paid. This is in addition to the already unfair wage gap reported between women and men. So, ladies, let's know our worth and negotiate. We may end up missing out when we don't ask for salary increases. The worst the decision makers could do is say, no. I am encouraging you from this day forward to negotiate your salary and pay increases.

Ladies let's know our worth and negotiate.

There are rules in negotiating salary and pay increases. The general rule is that the first person to suggest the salary figure during the negotiations loses the negotiation power. When you interview for a position, prepare to negotiate your salary, and do not take the first offer. I provide websites at the end of this chapter that you can use to leverage for salary ranges. These salaries are categorized by professions. Keep this information in your back pocket for when you are negotiating.

Men are expected to negotiate but women must operate in persuasiveness when negotiating for their salaries. It's not fair, but these are the current rules. Women are to be nice in all things. So, the answer is to be nice when you ask for a higher wage, but as Mary Sue Coleman, former president of University of Michigan calls it, be "relentlessly pleasant." Stay pleasant throughout the negotiations. This method requires smiling throughout the negotiations, finding common interests, and expressing appreciation. View the negotiation process as solving a problem. The problem you are solving is speaking up on behalf of others whether it is speaking for all women by negotiating for a pay increase or by speaking from a team perspective. For example, you may say, "We had an amazing data center implementation." Show that you are asking as part of the greater good for all women and be prepared to tell them why you are asking for a larger wage. Per Sheryl Sandberg, COO of Facebook, women (not men) must provide an explanation as to why they are asking for an increase. Preface your question of the wage increase by stating that you know that women often are paid less than men, so you are going to negotiate rather than accept the first offer. Also, you can ask what the salary range is for that role. These strategies remove the defense mechanism off the other person, because you are asking on behalf of all women so to speak.

When you negotiate for a pay increase, you can point out that you understand that jobs with "this level" of responsibility are compensated within "this pay range." Again, be nice and smile. Do not argue with anybody when it comes to negotiating salary. Do not argue with HR and do not argue with your boss. When you forcefully argue or push for pay increase or promotion, it rarely goes well.

If you do not receive the pay you wanted, do not leave the company only for the money. Oftentimes, you are not aware of the internal issues that are ongoing in the workplace where you are interviewing. Every organization puts their best foot forward when engaging candidates for hire. Search your heart and see if you have peace about leaving.

You can negotiate a salary increase for a lateral role. When I say lateral, I am referring to a role in a different area that is grouped within the same or similar pay band of your current role. Sometimes a lateral role may grow you and give you more opportunities to shine. Research the pay for the lateral position you are considering. Tell the hiring manager that it is your understanding that people in this role are paid within "x" pay range. If possible, have another senior level person negotiate your salary increase on your behalf. Senior level personnel and other hiring managers have history with HR when it comes to salary negotiations. Let that manager negotiate on your behalf. If applicable, give that senior level person or the other hiring manager a copy of the e.g., Robert Half salary report showing what the pay range is for a comparable role (see website to Robert Half).

Visit these sites to find out salary wages and ranges:
1. Salary.com – type in the job description and select it or whatever is close.

2. Roberthalf.com/salary guide – they have 6 different reports you can request by email. Those reports include: 1) Creative & Marketing, 2) Technology, 3) Office & Administrative, 4) Finance & Accounting, 5) Legal and 6) All.

3. View the company website where you applied to see if they list the salary range.

In summary, women must be bold, know our worth and negotiate our wages. We can negotiate and be "relentlessly pleasant" throughout the negotiation process.

8

Being a Woman in Corporate America

Women are as smart and powerful as men. However, we still face inequalities in the workplace and we know this. Some of these inequalities are linked to societal perceptions. We all have to deal with some level of unconscious bias. There can be unconscious bias of how men view women from a leadership perspective. There are also wrongful perceptions of how we as women view other women in leadership roles. Where did these disparities come from? They began during childhood. Boys are taught to explore and be superhuman, while girls are often taught to focus on looking cute and caring for their man. Although women are natural caregivers, we have more things we are wired to do. Women and girls should also be taught to take more risks, do more daring things and think bigger dreams.

Women typically have not been taught to expose ourselves (or our daughters) to fields that are dominated by men. Most of our toys are geared only toward being caregivers. Don't get me wrong, being a wife and mother are extremely important, but so is giving women opportunities to be leaders in their workplace. We are not trying to brute force our way into leadership, but rather, we want to be given the same opportunities presented to our male counterparts.

As women, we also must change how we see ourselves. We need to be confident in who we are. Oftentimes, a man will apply for a position and his background does not match the qualifications, but he is confident he can do the job. We also need to take more risks and apply for positions that do not match our background. If you think you could do it, apply for it!

We are seeing an uptick in women advancing and sitting in the top seats. The number of women CEOs on the Fortune 500 list hit an all-time record of 41. That is approximately 8% of all Fortune 500 leaders. This is encouraging as more men and women are stepping up to change the story for women. But we still have more work to do. Women and men leaders must continue to support women in upward mobility. Women also must mentor other women in their career aspirations as we keep making progressing and gaining the seats. I am optimistic about the progress that women are making in their fields. Women are resilience. Let's go ahead and dominate in all fields.

Here are keys to help us dominate our fields:

- *Hone your skills. Be the best in your field.*
- *Be confident in yourself and what you bring to the table.*
- *Find colleagues (women and men) that like and support you.*
- *Create solutions that will change your organization and your career*
- *Get to know the decision makers.*
- *Be the standard.*
- *Go for the big job. Don't fear success.*

When we see other women advancing, let's celebrate and support them. And when it's your turn and you advance, do the right thing. Help other women succeed.

9

Being Black in Corporate America

I am a woman and I am a black woman. Those two factors mean it is more challenging to break erroneous perceptions not only about women but women of color. Corporate America at least has gotten better about receiving us onto a team, but there are still barriers to overcome when it comes to being promoted. It is possible to be promoted, but there can be stricter guidelines and requirements when you are black or any woman of color. Nonetheless, we are making strides. Thankfully, not everyone in the workplace is purposefully biased or intends to be biased. So, we must guard our thoughts and hearts to remain positive. As Janet Marzett, retired VP of Mercedes-Benz, said, "Do not look for the bad in people. If you are always looking for the bad, you will find it."

> *"Do not look for the bad in people. If you are always looking for the bad, you will find it."*
> - JANET MARZETT, *retired Mercedes-Benz Financial Services, Vice President of Regional Operations*

Women of color must give special attention to how we are perceived and how we are being received. How a woman of color communicates is huge! It can make or break our opportunities. When communicating, pay attention to the body language of your colleagues. This will tell a lot about how you are being received. Also, this is important, watch your tone. Sometimes we women of various ethnic groups communicate in a louder fashion or should I say "urban" fashion. This could mean that sometimes people at work just don't get us and sometimes we may be misunderstood. I am not recommending that you change who you are, be authentic, but if you tend to be loud and direct, be a softer loud on the job. As colleagues get to experience more of your greatness, they will understand you better. In my opinion, I believe most successful people of color have a guard up, to a certain extent, when it comes to expressing their whole selves in corporate America. There is a trust factor involved and I am not saying to be fake, but we need to consider our audience.

We all need confidence and that includes women too. Everyone must have some level of confidence, even if they have to pretend to have it. My favorite story about exhibiting confidence comes from my former colleague Jeff. Jeff shared with me his experience working with one of our consultants at the time. Mitch was our consultant and he had a problem. Mitch did not understand one of our key business processes and how it worked. Jeff was empathetic and privately explained the entire process to Mitch. In just a few hours later, Mitch repackaged what he learned from Jeff, put it in a PowerPoint slide and confidently presented the key business process to our senior management. In fact, Mitch acted as if he were the expert on this topic the entire time. Exuding confidence is part of a consultant's personal brand. And we should all exhibit confidence in who we are and what we do. But displaying confidence can be tricky. Sometimes when you are confident, your confidence may be misconstrued as overly confident. What does it mean to be overly confident? I think it means to be prideful, arrogant and/or in need of more professional growth. Being viewed as overly confident can hurt your brand, so if or when it does happen, you have to manage that perception. Your confidence is not something that you give up. However, it must be properly conveyed.

Being a Christian, I believe God created all people as equal. I see myself as being equal with everyone else and I politely expect and require equal treatment in the workplace. Society must catch up to this truth. However, I do believe when all of us persevere in our purpose and work, we eventually receive our rewards.

There are some labels we must prove to be wrong. There is the misguided label that black women are angry. I believe many times it is not that we are angry, but we are frustrated. We strive and desire to be our authentic selves at work. However, sometimes what people want is for us to be and act like what they want to see. Plus, we are not always allowed to show emotion at work, but to be honest, we all should work on how we manage our emotions. Sis, when you receive an unpleasant response from someone, here is a good response exercise from Dr. Caroline Leaf: Before reacting, close your eyes and imagine the wisest, most loving version of yourself and how they would or would not respond. Open your eyes and do that. Now, I will admit that this takes some practice. If you don't close your eyes, still take that deep breath, and pause before you speak. If you are not in a safe place to "be you" at work, put a guard over your mouth, and your emotions. Lock yourself in a bathroom stall until you feel okay or wait until you get home to unleash your frustrations. Alternatively, take your cell phone, leave the work area, and find a private spot where you can vent. Talk to a friend, family member or seek counseling. Make healthy choices to preserve your peace. One time, I was sitting in a meeting that Kathy, a lead manager, was facilitating. My cell phone vibrated. It was an important call, so I stepped out of that meeting to answer it. What I heard on the call was that someone had broken into my rental property and had stolen everything. This was thousands of dollars lost. I was distraught, but I ended the call and rushed back into the meeting. After the meeting, I hung around to talk to Kathy. She and I had a good relationship. Kathy liked my work so I had asked her if she would write a comment I could put in my personal file. Kathy went on to tell me that she noticed my mood had changed when I had returned to the earlier meeting. When I tried to explain to her that I had gotten some bad news, she went on to say that I needed to control my emotions. 'Wow,' I thought. Can black women or any women show any emotion other than happiness at work? Sometimes, the answer is "no." Although, we may be happy most of the time, we have bad days too. Black women and other women of color often are not given permission to share or show our emotions at work. This can be disheartening, but in those bad days, we must guard our hearts and our responses.

> *"Before reacting, close your eyes and imagine the wisest, most loving version of yourself and how they would or would not respond. Open your eyes and do that."*
> - DR. CAROLINE LEAF

There are times when you may need to have crucial conversations about how you feel, about your career and how your advancement is going. In those times, be honest, remain respectful and know your worth. Even still, you must evaluate when it is time to leave an assignment. If you feel tolerated and not celebrated, have conversations with your supervisor, manager, coaches and other leaders that are vested in your success. Then strategically/prayerfully decide whether or not it is time to look for another work opportunity or stay and tough it out. Bishop T.D Jakes said, "The right thing at the wrong time will lead to failure."

> *"The right thing at the wrong time will lead to failure."*
> - BISHOP JAKES

Gaining and receiving supporters is not color nor gender specific. Recognize those people and connect. Maybe one or more of them can mentor you or help you push upward. Get to know the decision makers in your organization without being phony. Many of these decision makers are open to mentor you, but you don't know if you don't ask. If they say yes, you drive the discussions, agendas, and meetings. Let the first meeting or two be about getting to know each other personally. Grow your relationships, operate in mutual respect, invest in yourself and allow people who see your potential to deposit into your development. Mentor and help develop others as well. No one succeeds without help from other people. When you have faith, nothing or no one can stop you from becoming who you were made to be.

10

How to Identify Why You Are Here and Your Purpose

If we take a step back from the busyness of life, we recognize there is a yearning to know why we are here and for what purpose. Another fundamental truth is that we are not here by accident. It is not even possible to be here by accident. If you look at our world and everything in it, everything has a purpose. For example, look at everything in your house, each thing has a purpose. I remember when I was in high school, my dad decided it was time I learned how to repair a tire. My dad was extremely handsome, a Georgian, born and raised in the south. He left the south and came to Michigan. He worked in an assembly plant for one of the major automotive companies. Everybody in our neighborhood loved him because he was always dripping with southern charm. He waived and spoke to everyone. Sometimes people were skeptical of his intentions. But dad did not know how to be anyone other than who he was, which was a friendly and kind person. I was in high school when dad decided it was time for me to learn how to change a flat tire. I had my own car and Dad did not want me out somewhere stranded because I did not know how to repair a tire. Most of the time, dad was just a phone call away, but he still wanted me to have this skill. So, dad started me on tire training on a lovely, spring day in Detroit. There I was, 16 years old, ready and willing to learn how to repair a flat tire. Dad started by positioning bricks under the car as a safety precaution, in the unlikely event that the jack would slip out of place. Dad then grabbed the jack out of the trunk of my car. Then he began to raise the car with the jack. He had the tool kit positioned by the car. One of the first steps involved removing the wheel nuts. This is where purpose came in. There is a tool created for removing these wheel nuts and it is called a lug wrench. I watched dad put his muscle into each turn of his hand to loosen each lug. This looked hard. I remember thinking, 'I hope I am never called upon to repair a tire.' When dad loosened the wheel nuts, I took over to complete the removal of the wheel nuts and the tire. A screwdriver or hammer has its own purpose and neither of these tools was created to remove tire lugs. Just like any tool, purchase, or anything else, they all have a purpose and we do too!

So how do you recognize your purpose?

There are several ways to identify why you are here:
1. Through your work assignments at your workplace – look for the passion
2. By re-examining your childhood passions, behaviors, likes and dislikes
3. By asking God in prayer
4. By motivational gifts

To Answer, "Why am I here?" Let's Look at Your Work Assignments

If I were to ask you how you feel about your job, what adjectives would you use to describe your feelings? Are you happy or unhappy with your work? Are you just there for a paycheck? In my decades of life in corporate America, I have seen some miserable people. I know for sure many of us are working in jobs we either hate or tolerate! This is not good. Not recognizing "why am I here?" is a major reason for people's unhappiness. One of the reasons I am pouring out my heart to you and sharing my story through this book, is to help you find out why you are here. Do you like the work that you are doing? Do you have passion for your work? Sometimes we only kind of like what we are doing. Other times we have talent, but it is raw talent, and it needs development.

For example, let's look at Michael Jordan in his youth. Michael Jordan was kicked off the basketball team in high school because his skill was not developed. He worked on his game that following summer and the rest is history as he eventually went on to international fame. He had natural talent, but he needed to develop it. Your purpose is tied to your natural gifts and talents. For a long time, I did not know to look for purpose in my work. When we do not see purpose in our work, we are not fulfilled. When you do not know your purpose or you are in the wrong job, unhappiness is bound to show up. It will show up in these ways:

- *Dull work/life routines - E.g., get up, grab your coffee, go to work, eat, sleep, repeat*
- *Inability to succeed*
- *Clock watching at work*
- *Mediocrity*
- *Low self-esteem, low achievement, and poor performance*
- *Worry*
- *Depression*

The opposite is true when you feel connected to your work and sense purpose in it and these outcomes show up:

- *Focus*
- *Success*
- *Higher self-esteem and personal achievement*

- *Fulfillment*
- *Happiness*
- *Greater energy and productivity*
- *Better life*
- *Tangible rewards*

There are many benefits in knowing your purpose and being in the right job. Once I learned to look for purpose, I started looking for purpose through my work. Do you have raw talent that needs development? Do you have passion for the work that you do? If you answered yes to these questions, you are probably fulfilling your purpose.

"If you can't figure out your purpose, figure out your passion. For your passion will lead you into your purpose." - T.D. JAKES

Re-examining your childhood passions, behaviors, likes and dislikes:

Sometimes it takes a visit back to our childhoods for us to see and recognize our talents. Our purposes, gifts and talents are pre-planted in our DNA.

God pre-planted our purpose, gifts, and talents in our DNA.

And some of us are not enjoying our work life because we don't understand our purpose. We are on the wrong path, headed in the wrong direction. Others need clarity. What are your gifts and talents? What are those things that naturally peak your interest? I encourage you right now to take some time to explore things about yourself. Revisit your childhood right now if you can or schedule it so that you'll do it! Things that get scheduled get done.

Let's revisit your childhood right now if you can or schedule it so that you'll do it! Things that get scheduled get done.

Pick a quiet place and begin to journal. Write down childhood passions, behaviors, likes and dislikes. Be sure to write down those things or activities that brought you joy.

Journaling helped me to validate my purpose. I did exactly what I am encouraging you to do. I wrote out my childhood interests and it helped lead me to my why.

Here are some of my discoveries from journaling my childhood:

- I loved math. It came easy to me.
- I loved reconciling the grocery bill by adding figures in my head.
- I charged my parents for chores I did around the house
- I enjoyed saving money in my piggy bank..
- I made pot holders as a child with my sister and sold them door to door.
- In high school, I sold donuts to classmates.

In just this one exercise, I realized I had a thing for money. I grew up in a household of five girls. Oh, my dear dad! How did he survive with six women (my mom included) in the house? We all had chores but let my sisters tell it, I did not have nearly the chores they did. One day, I decided to clean up the entire house from the top floors to the basement. As I cleaned, I created a fee schedule for each service. When my dad came home from work, I was so excited. I could not wait to share my invoice with him and my mom. It was a detailed list of all the chores I completed and the associated fees I was charging for each service. Sweeping the floor, $2, washing the windows, $2, folding the laundry $3. I was so proud of myself and exuberant about the money I was going to make. I looked on as they read my invoice.

But to my surprise, to my parents did not pay me a single dime. I was upset! My parents just laughed it off. That was a clue into my future purpose.

There were other moments in my childhood that pointed me toward purpose. I remember while watching television with my sisters, I asked them a question. "How much do we pay for television?"

They both looked at me confused. This was the early '70s and TV was free. "No one pays for television. The advertisers pay a fee to broadcast their commercials. Those fees cover the cost of television and that's why we do not have to pay," my sister said.

I was just eight years old, but I remember thinking this would one day be monetized." I am still mad that I was not one of the pioneers of cable television because I saw it coming. Even then I had a mind for business.

WHEN LIFE HAPPENS:

There are some moments in our childhood that change us forever. They influence our make-up, our personality and who we become. There is a day like that tattooed in my mind that I could never forget. It started so normal. I was 11 years old. Back then days consisted of playing outside with my friends from morning to night. We played tag, rode bikes and climbed trees outside until the street lights came on.

One summer day, my mom left for her routine checkup at the doctor's office. After running a few tests, the doctor suggested that she stay overnight and have a procedure done. It was nothing major, but she would need to stay in the hospital for a few days. My dad took me and my siblingto visit her in the hospital, and I regaled her with all the chores I had completed around the house, hoping I could earn a little extra allowance and bonus points when she returned home. Later, we said our goodbyes for the night and left for home.

The next day, the phone rang in the distance. Dad answered the phone. It was the hospital. As he hung up, he and my sisters began scurrying around and left in haste for the hospital. I sat alone in my room, a little afraid about what all this meant. I tried to occupy my mind with my paper dolls, but I started to grow anxious. Then suddenly, I heard the front door swing open and my oldest sister stormed up the stairs and into her bedroom. I was in the room adjacent to hers with my door closed and thought to myself, 'what is that sound I'm hearing?' Is she crying? Then dad opened my door and entered my room. He sat down on my bed gently as if there were pin needles protruding from the bed. My big brown eyes were focused attentively on him now and I heard nothing else as I looked at him. He looked at me with such tenderness. and honestly, and said softly, "Mom has died."

He could not hold back the tears any longer and he sobbed loudly. It was in that moment, the pain of hearing these words was indescribable. I experienced so much grief in that moment that I could not speak. I immediately went into shock and this once vibrant little girl went into a cocoon. That part of my life was a dark patch in the tapestry of my heart. My mom was our world, and we did not function well without her. We went to counseling for a while and tried picking up the pieces, but I was forever changed. Being raised by my dad, I missed out on some of the social graces that come with being raised by a woman: how to be lady-like, how to carry yourself, how to interact with the opposite sex. My mom was an amazing cook, but I never learned any of her recipes. I still wish I could recreate her flawless sweet potato pie recipe. I was left to figuring out womanhood on my own. Overtime, I grew to be strong and independent. I had to be. Don't get me wrong, my dad was the best kind of father and I learned a lot from him. He taught me work ethic and discipline. He worked on the assembly line at Ford Motor Company and woke up early enough to arrive at the plant an hour before his shift began. He was never late and he never missed a day of work. I know who he was impacted who I became. And although it was devastating losing my mom, the experience helped shape me into who I am today.

"You can still win in life and fulfill your purpose when life happens."

There were other moments in my childhood that pointed me to purpose. As a kid, I loved math, especially addition. When I went to the grocery store with my sister, I always took a sheet of paper and a pen so that I could add up the cost of all the grocery items. For every item my sister placed in the basket, I tallied up the cost. Most of the time, when all our purchases were wrung up, my hand calculated total would match the register total, right down to the penny. Oh, how much I loved that! How many children do you know that get excited about numbers or money like this? Answer: Children who are born with these types of gifts and talents for accounting, business, or finance. To experience happiness in the workplace, these are the types of areas I needed to pursue.

When I went to college, I selected Wayne State over another school because I did not like the big university feel. Wayne State is a good school, but what I did not know was what to major in. I did not have a mentor or good counselor to help me with these decisions. The funny thing is that I initially pursued a Business Administration degree not because I connected the dots to my purpose. I chose Business Administration because that was my older sister Patty's major. These are the kinds of things we do when we do not understand our purpose. I began leaning into what turned out to be my natural talents. God and his mercy were guides.

The curriculum for the Business School at Wayne State required that you took classes in accounting, management, marketing, and finance. None of these disciplines were offered at my high school, and we had no college level courses. So, I was not familiar with the foundational concepts of accounting and when I took my first accounting class, I lacked confidence. My accounting professor, on the other hand, was quite confident in himself. He walked with confidence and dressed in flair. He was tall, middle aged, olive skin, with gray and dark brown hair. As I studied for the exam, I practiced preparing journal entries and financial statements because this was going to be a major part of the exam. However, as I sat in the class during the exam, something happened that I had never experienced. I froze during the exam and started second guessing what I was doing. When I got my exam back, my grade was a "D." The truth was, I really did understand accounting, I just lacked confidence. When I looked at my graded exam, I knew exactly what I had done wrong and so I went to talk to the professor. He told me all was not lost and that if I did well on the final, I could still get a "C" out of the class. I asked him if I got an A on the final if he would give me a B out of the class. Instead, his response was:

"If you get 100%, I will give you a B."

So, what did I do? I studied to try to get 100%. On the final exam, we once again had to prepare journal entries and financial statements. We had to do all of this by hand. This accounted for 40% of our exam grade. The other 60% of the test was multiple choice. When I got my test results back, my journal entries and financial statements were perfect with no errors! But, I missed a few of the multiple-choice questions. I went to see the professor and I asked him if he would give me the "B" I felt I earned, but he said "no." I finished my first accounting class with a "C." But I knew I had done better than what my grade showed. I discovered zeal and passion for accounting, and I was determined to finish the business school curriculum. I also made these discoveries:

- I had a natural talent for accounting

- I had passion for accounting

And as I continued through college, I realized I liked management too.

- I had a natural gifting for management

- I had passion for management

If you haven't already, it is time for you to look back at your childhood passions, behaviors, likes and dislikes. You may also want to look at some of your childhood sayings as well. What were you like as a kid? What kind of things did you enjoy doing? What about those teenage years? What were you like in college? Let's discover your personal gifts and talents together. Take a window of time where you can separate yourself from your phone or anything that can distract you.

Take this time for yourself and journal your childhood to discover your gifts and talents. You will find the emotion that accompanies your gifts and talents is passion! As Oprah says: "Passion is energy. Feel the power that comes from focusing on what excites you."

> *"Passion is energy. Feel the power that comes from focusing on what excites you."* -OPRAH WINFREY

FINDING YOUR PURPOSE – Taking a look back at your childhood
- Ask your family what common themes they noticed about you when you were a kid (verbal and non-verbal), your behavior patterns, your interests - write those down.

- Journal out everything you liked to do as a kid.
  Think back to when you were little – what naturally peaked your interest? What kind of things did you like doing? What were some things you daydreamed about or wanted to do? Visualize and think back to what things you would say and do as a child. Look for behavior patterns and interests. Do not feel bad if you cannot remember everything. What you are wired to do does not become apparent to you all at once. It is revealed in increments and it takes time. It is like pieces to your life puzzle. You will understand more and more over time, but you need to start the process of identifying them.

- Write down things about your personality or behavior you remember then and now.
- Write down the subjects you liked in school.
- Write down phrases and comments you used to make.
- Write down sports, books, movies, arts you liked.
- Write down activities you succeeded in.
- Write down what your playtime was like.
- Write down what you thought was fun.
- Write down early work experiences, summer jobs.

And finally, List the gifts and talents you realize you have.

What surprised you?

Now, look at what you are currently doing in the workplace.
- Does your career or work have any correlation to your gifts and talents?
- Does your current job reflect, or career path reflect any of these characteristics?

Identifying Your Child's Purpose

If you are a parent or future parent, we can take this process a step further. Parents, pay attention to what interests your children. Those talents are going to make themselves known, but you must be on the lookout for them. As you look for where your children's interest naturally gravitates to, you will see them acting out their gifts and talents.

Go ahead and journal your children's behaviors. Each child is different, so journal about each of them separately.

Congratulations on taking these steps to help guide your child in their destiny.

What about older children? Parents, you can also help them find their purpose through praying, observing, and journaling. It is never too late.

For example, my daughter Jill loved singing when she was a kid, and she had a beautiful voice. She would confidently and boldly enter singing contests. At the age of 8 or 9, she started writing songs. I paid for piano lessons and bought her a keyboard she could practice on. Jill faithfully attended her piano classes for weeks. However, after a while it became clear that she was over it. She did not have a bad attitude, she just realized that she did not like it.

When Jill turned 19, I gave her a surprise birthday party, and someone bought her an acoustic guitar as a present. To my surprise, Jill loved that acoustic guitar. She started strumming it and it was instantly clear that she had a natural talent. In fact, she taught herself to play. At the age of 25, Jill wrote, published, and produced her own album as an independent artist! And since then, Jill (Govan) has published an EP and other projects. As a parent, I am happy that she followed her passion. She did not cave into the pressure of onlookers and well-meaning mentors. She is a singer, songwriter, and musician! That is what she loves, and she is great at it!

Parents, please do not push off your dreams and unfulfilled desires on your children. Give them space to find out their gifting and talents without applying pressure to manipulate their purpose. If you are a future parent, you want to give your children as many engaging experiences as you can so that you can help them identify their gifts and talents. Give them opportunities in creative spaces, opportunities to place sports, visit museums, and explore science, technology, engineering, mathematics and so on. Also, take your children on local and national trips. If possible, take them out of the country. Give them an opportunity to explore various roles while visiting and/or introducing them to work. These exposures play a major role in helping your children identify their gifts and talents.

Seek mentors to help cultivate their gifts.

My sincere hope is that each of you will find the courage to follow your passion and what excites you. This will lead you to your purpose and a more fulfilled life!

For those of you who are Christians:

God planned your purpose before you were born. You just need to be able to hear what He's saying about your purpose. You can learn your purpose by praying and asking God about it. You may need to set aside focused prayer time on this topic. Prayer is one of the ways you can hear from God. Another way to hear from God is to read your bible. God speaks through His scriptures. I find reading the scriptures out loud to be helpful, because faith comes by hearing.

We learn facets of our purpose throughout our life's journey. Do not be discouraged and don't expect to know everything about your purpose at once. However, be excited about your life and purpose because as Pastor André Butler says, "God has a future for you. And your future is bright."

> *"God has a future for you. And your future is bright."*
> -PASTOR ANDRÉ BUTLER

Finding Your Purpose Through Gifts

Gifts – Take the quiz at Gifttest.org

God has given us gifts for doing things well. These gifts are mentioned in the bible, in Romans 12:6-8. There are 7 gifts:

1. Perceiver
   - They have a keen sense of right and wrong. They have an intense disdain for injustice. They apply their convictions to everyday life.

   - Their role is to reveal information to help others.

- They often appear direct, blunt, or inconsiderate, but sincerely want to help.
- They are often their own worst critics, perfectionists, and are often misunderstood.

2. Server
    - They provide for material, spiritual, or physical needs of others.
    - They take care of the less fortunate in society.
    - They may feel personally rejected if their offer of help is rejected.
    - They are efficient and keep things moving.

3. Teacher
    - They use sound, rational, and instructive reasoning to convince and help others to learn.
    - They tend to be talkative.
    - They are avid debaters.
    - They usually love research and the opportunity to share what they have learned.

4. The Encourager
    - They edify and exhort.
    - They speak messages of encouragement.
    - They bring joy and comfort but can be offended when people are inconsiderate.
    - They work well with all personalities.

5. The Giver
    - They are generous and have a charitable nature.
    - They specifically contribute to the less fortunate.

- They give of their excess to those who have nothing.
- They sacrifice to give of their time and self.

6. The Ruler/Leader
   - They can see the "big picture".
   - They move everyone toward a common goal.
   - They set good examples and provide sound counsel.
   - They can bring order by setting up structures, systems, and methods for others to follow.

7. Showing Mercy
   - They are compelled to have passion for people.
   - They help people in misery.
   - They demonstrate a large amount of patience.
   - They are the first to listen and sympathize when someone is suffering.

I encourage you to go ahead and take the test at Gifttest.org. This test will show you primary and secondary motivational gifts. Learning these motivational gifts will aid you both in your purpose (gifts and callings) and in everyday life communication with others.

The quality of your life is partly predicated upon knowing your purpose and being in the right work spaces. Don't get discouraged if you don't have it all figured out, because none of us do. But get on the path to learning your purpose and be committed to the work you are already doing. As you continue to seek those answers and put the things we discussed here in motion, you will find your path. You will fulfill your purpose.

11

Girl Boss

It was a cold Friday afternoon in Michigan and I was preparing to go on vacation. Michigan is so beautiful in the winter when it snows. I was sitting at my desk when I received a text from my prior boss.

She said, "Karen, that opportunity I was telling you about has just opened. Are you still interested?"

At first, I thought to myself, 'what opportunity?' Then it clicked; she had told me an opportunity in Information Security may come up, but we had not talked about this in months. I responded to the text with a "yes." I had no idea as to what I was signing up for. Marcie (we will call her) told me that the Information Security Officer for one of our affiliate companies was taking a leave for three months, and they needed someone to fill that role on an interim basis. This company's office was in Atlanta and I lived in Michigan. They were in crisis mode and needed this help immediately. I would soon find out that it was a far greater crisis than I thought. The affiliate company wanted me to come live in Georgia for three months, provide strategic direction, run their day-to-day operations, lead their information security team, and close their audit findings. Not only did they need help but my current boss in Michigan also wanted me to continue carrying out my existing responsibilities as well. It was a daunting task, but I was willing to take the risk.

Marcie went on to tell me that this was a high-profile role and that I would report to the CIO and be in meetings with senior management on a regular basis. I thought, 'cool,' although I was a little nervous. If I did well, this could be a big win for my career, but if I did not do well, this could be a setback.

I got approval from my CIO and left within three days to embark on this journey. Jennie, the person I would be covering for, was supposed to catch me up before she left on personal leave, but she was hard to get a hold of. When I finally reached her, she asked, "So, what do you know about what's going on here?"

I said, "I don't know a whole lot about it, but I'll be flying in."

She was shocked and responded as if to say, "Why would you take a position when you don't know the state of the affairs?" But, I learned to be a risk taker. And I recognize the best rewards come from taking the highest risks.

I learned to be a risk taker. And I recognize the best rewards come from taking the highest risks.

Where did I get this "risk taker courage" from? It came from working places as a consultant and having to think quickly on my feet. It came from learning to hone my skills and training to be a Certified Public Accountant. It came from self-study and being willing to leave my comfort zone to put myself out there. It came from knowing what I wanted was not just going to be handed to me.

I arrived in Atlanta in the early evening and my adrenaline was going. I caught a metro car from the airport to the office to meet up with the CIO's managing assistant. Everything was going according to plan. I had booked a hotel close to the office, so all I needed to do was get there, grab some dinner, and get a good night's rest. I arrived early to the hotel and went to the front desk to check in. As I approached the counter and showed my ID, the hotel manager said, "Oh I am so sorry, we are booked." She told me that this was the first night of a major sales convention. All the hotels in the Atlanta area were sold out. 'Okay,' I thought, but that should not have been my problem because I had booked this hotel in advance. The short answer was, they had given up my room to a convention goer and had changed my reservation without telling me. They had rebooked me in a room at one of their sister hotels, somewhere up the road.

Fortunately, the hotel manager was thinking on her feet. She told me that my night's stay would be free to accommodate for my inconvenience. Most times when people have provided poor customer service, I have required some form of compensation for my inconvenience, and over 90% of the time these companies have accommodated me. You do not have to yell or mistreat people; you just share with them the value of your time. Your time is precious. It has intrinsic value, and when people waste your time, you should be compensated.

> ***Your time is precious. It has intrinsic value, and when people waste your time, you should be compensated.***

The next day, I pulled up to the office building and wow! It looked impressive. Newly constructed, nice! It was built with new workspace concepts; coffee bar, private rooms, and a full fitness center. I walked in dressed to impress. I met the colleagues on my team, and they seemed wonderful. I would lead a staff of three employees and four contractors. Shortly afterward, I met with Diane, the CIO. She was cordial and "dressed to impress."

She said, "Karen, I want you to get situated and comfortable, but I also want the work done."

I told her that I understood. She then took me to meet the other senior leaders. I was then whisked into a conference room with her and the president of the Company. The president was very cordial but said, "Do not expect to just leave, now that you are here and we need your help."

I chuckled and thought, 'okay, no pressure I see.' After the meeting, Diane sent out an email communication with my biography to the entire organization. She bragged on me and told everyone to give me their full support. That is what I loved most about Diane.

I want to take a moment to speak again about women supporting other women. Diane was not threatened by me, but rather supported me. Too many of us do not support each other. Each woman should pull up another woman.

I returned to my desk where I began to dig into things to gain an understanding of what needed to be done. I had not received a good knowledge transfer from the predecessor, and she was now on personal leave. I met with my team to get a status of what was urgent (on fire) and to learn their roles. I put my consultant hat on, researched and worked with a sense of urgency. I plowed through documents, emails, and identified work "fires." I was focused and determined to get a handle on things. I worked and worked, and the next thing I knew it was 9:45 pm. I had arrived early, worked through lunch, and now it was 9:45 pm. I do not condone working these kinds of long hours over an extended period. However, I was on an out-of-town mission and I needed results!

The office was quiet now and I thought I was the only person there. Then suddenly, I heard Diane.

She said, "Karen, what are you doing still here?"

I said, "I'm leaving soon." But she was still there too! Diane and I were the last two standing. Diane left and I followed at 10:30 pm.

It was day nine in Atlanta, and I was still living out of a suitcase. This time in a different hotel. The eventual plan was for me to move into an apartment close by. I arrived at the office in a cheerful mood. As I walked into the work area, I noticed Jonathan. He was one of my colleagues on my team. Jonathan was a very knowledgeable, kind-hearted, hard-working individual. He would prove to be a 'ride or die' colleague who stayed late many nights to help me resolve problems and get things in order. But, at this time, I could see he was stressed. I could hear his heavy breathing.

I said, "Jonathan, what's wrong?"

He proceeded to tell me the plan my predecessor had for closing their audit findings. My predecessor had left Jonathan in charge of tracking all the audit findings and corresponding remediation plans. I asked Jonathan to share this Excel document with me that had all the audit findings and remediation plans. When I opened the spreadsheet, it was clear why Jonathan was stressed. Somehow 15 IT audit findings and the courses of action to take had morphed into 100s of lines of data. There were lines upon lines of information to digest. Included in this Excel spreadsheet were meeting notes, recommendations, and policies without any decent connectivity. There were numerous documented comments to decipher. It also was difficult to identify the solutions that were supposed to address closing the audit issues and time was of the essence. It was vitally important that these audit issues were remediated and closed this year. The remediation of these security audit findings was the top priority of the president, CIO, and senior management, and the expectation was that solutions would be found to remedy all 15 issues by the end of this year. However, the question was, how were we going to get through all this data, recommendations and verify the solutions to implement? Based on my observations, some of the remediations provided were not appropriate to close the sited audit issues. It was at that point I realized that the President and senior management had no idea how behind things were and that the audit plan and audit remediations cited were in a lot of ways, nonsensical.

That afternoon, I accompanied the senior leaders to a meeting with the president. At that meeting, the president stated that once the audit remediation plans were finalized, he wanted to review them. I sat there thinking about the mess I was left with. There was no way the president was going to be able to make any sense out of the existing audit remediation plans. After the meeting, I went back to my desk. I opened the Excel document once more. I proceeded to read through lines upon lines of data and I was overwhelmed. I had a firsthand view of what was stressing Jonathan out, and the information was changing all the time. It was a nightmare to understand and manage. I needed to take a bold stand and come up with a new plan to share with the CIO. That afternoon, I had my 1:1 with Diane.

I looked her square in the eye and I said, "Diane, I cannot execute the audit remediation plan that I have inherited. The plan is discombobulated with 100s of lines of Excel comments. I am going to throw out this plan and start over from scratch. I will meet with the audit issue owners. I will interview them while having a project manager present. I will help identify the solutions to close these audit issues, and as we identify these solutions during these meetings, I will have the project manager document them in our project tool."

I told her the truth but also provided solutions for how to effectively accomplish the goal of timely closure of these audit findings. The result was that she was blown away by my answer and my approach.

As I met with some of the stakeholders, they were initially resistant. However, after meeting and working closely with them, I gained their confidence. I believe this happened because I was "sold out" for helping them resolve their issues and everyone saw it. I had passion and zeal. I dug in and collaborated with my security team, presidents, senior management, application and infrastructure management teams and consultants. We identified solutions to all of the audit findings. I was able to successfully lead strategic initiatives, the IT security team and IT operations. And with the support and input from my team, I was able to lead the charge for timely implementation of remediation plans for closure of all of the audit issues. Sustainability for a more robust and secure IT landscape was also being formed. The crisis had been abated and expectations exceeded.

At the end of this assignment, here is what the president of their company had to say in an email to my company president, global CIO, regional CIO, and my boss.

Hello Pete (president) and Rob (global CIO)

We would like to express our sincere appreciation to Karen Hoskin. She took on a short-term assignment in Atlanta as the interim Information Security Officer and Department Manager starting from 15 Jan until the end of March. Her assignment was confirmed on 12 January and she made herself available immediately on such a short notice. Karen as a Certified Information Security Manager and Certified Public Accountant became a tremendous support for our company with her background and experience about company information security and audit. From day one, she highly contributed to our process conformity projects together with the IT senior management team along with information security teams. Her pleasant personality and excellent communication skills also helped to engage all the stakeholders and team members. We are already seeing a vast improvement in engagement of stakeholders and progress of remediation.

Both our organizations identified information security as the top collaboration areas last year and this case became a great example of collaboration between our Companies in North America. We also appreciate your CIO to make such an outclass available for the last months.

We would like to express our deep gratitude to Karen and wish her a successful career in the company. We are looking forward to more collaboration in the future!

This letter was much appreciated. This level of acknowledgment was and is exceptional. It was a great personal accomplishment and I am thankful. I took a risk uprooting my life and relocating to Atlanta for this assignment. It was a hefty risk as I took a leap of faith, but the risk I took was worth it!

Here are some keys for career empowerment:

- *Hone your skills.*
- *Be strategic, providing solutions to business problems and challenges.*
- *Own your career – take charge, be in charge.*
- *Work hard.*
- *Take risks.*
- *Be so awesome that your skills are sought after.*
- *Learn the 7 Principles to Empower You in the Workplace up next.*

12

7 Principles to Empower You in the Workplace

I am so excited to share these 7 principles with you that will empower you in the workplace! This information comes from my years of work experiences, trial and error and coaching by C-suiters. These principles are aimed at giving you wisdom and foresight to catapult your career and to give you the career you've dreamed of.

PRINCIPLE #1 – Six Habits of Powerful People

Our daily habits and pursuits determine our successes as well as our failures; therefore, we need to develop habits to ensure our daily and long term successes. Studies have shown that powerful people share similar habits that have propelled them in their pursuit of excellence. I want to share six of those habits with you.

To operate at the same level as some of the most powerful people in the world, you need to incorporate these habits:

1. Pursuit of excellence in your work.
2. Be an early riser - with daily devotion and meditation.
3. Exercise 3 to 6 days a week.
4. Schedule daily and weekly goals.
5. Pursuit of continuous learning.
6. Tell your story.

Habit #1 Pursuit of Excellence in Your Work

The first habit, pursuit of excellence in your work starts with performing work that you are passionate about, that is, the work that peaks your interest! It's the work that excites you! Steve Jobs said, "Your work is going to fill a large part of your life, and the only way to be truly satisfied is to do what you believe is great work." Everyone needs to feel like the work they are doing matters. That's why it is imperative that you know your purpose and the type of work that excites you. It is hard to build a career when you're doing work that you have no zeal for.

How you approach your work impacts the outcome of your success. If your approach to work has little to no zeal, your level of success will also have little to no impact. Steve Jobs said, " Be a yardstick of quality. Some people aren't used to an environment where excellence is expected."

> *"Your work is going to fill a large part of your life, and the only way to be truly satisfied is to do what you believe is great work."* -STEVE JOBS

> *"I don't know what my calling is, but I want to be here for a bigger reason. I strive to be like the greatest people who ever lived."* -WILL SMITH

Here are some questions to ask yourself to gauge your interest in the work you currently doing:
1. How do you see yourself changing your world for the better?
2. What is your dream?
3. What do you love learning about?
4. At the end of your life, what would you like to look back on and say I did it?
5. What is it that keeps you up at night because you are excited?

Find the work you enjoy and do it. I discuss in Chapter 10, how to identify why you are here and your purpose.

> *"Be a yardstick of quality. Some people aren't used to an environment where excellence is expected."*
> -STEVE JOBS

You want to develop your own mission statement. Write down how you want to build your career, what training you need to develop your skills and what you are looking to achieve. Answer these questions: what do I want to achieve and what do I want to be remembered for in my life, my work, my career and my organization. This is your mission statement. Also, as the captain of your career, you must steer it and manage it. Throughout your career, you will need to develop and invest in your development. Identify coaches who will are willing to pour into your career. Communicate your career goals and aspirations work with your supervisors and coaches.

Opportunities will present themselves during your career. You will get opportunities to showcase your skills, talents, savvy, and ability. My question to you is will you be ready? Whatever your current role is in your organization, operate in a state of readiness. Do not let someone catch you slacking in knowing your area of responsibility or lacking in preparedness or foresight.

My follow-up question is, what is the level of excellence you put into your work? When you complete a work assignment, do you just do the bare minimum of what is required? Do not do this, but instead, go ahead and "hit the ball out of the park." Work hard and play hard. Exceed your boss and other stakeholder's expectations!

Bishop T.D. Jakes said, "Too many people want the appearance of winning rather than the practices and hard work that create a true champion."

Habit #2 Be an early riser - with daily devotion and meditation.

The second habit of powerful people is to be an early riser. Take advantage of the early part of your day to secure an impactful day. Mark Zuckerberg, Jack Ma and Jeff Bezos are leaders who start their day early in the morning. Jeff Bezos says, "Go to bed early and wake up early." I like to rise at 6:00 am and spend 6:00-7:30 am daily, reading my bible, meditating and praying. This habit helps me relax and gives me clarity.

Habit #3 Exercise 3 to 6 days a week.

The third habit of powerful individuals is to exercise. Exercise 3 to 6 days a week. I typically exercise from 7:45 to 8:30 am 3 to 5 days a week. Exercise reduces stress and feelings of depression. It releases endorphins which triggers a positive feeling in your body and energizes how you look at life. Exercise helps you to be positive, calm and have clear thoughts to start your day. It promotes a healthy body and a healthy mind set. Per Kim Kardashian, "It's important to work out and be the best version of yourself that you can be, but never feel like you have to be the skinniest girl in the room to be the prettiest." Jennifer Lopez said, "Sometimes when I get home and I'm not feeling so great, I make myself go to the gym. Then I come home and take a shower, put on a great outfit, some makeup, tie my hair up, and I feel pepped up and great about myself."

Habit #4 Schedule daily and weekly goals.

Schedule out your goals and tasks for the day and the week. You can do this at the beginning or end of your day. Many powerful people do their scheduling the night before. When you schedule your assignments, goals, or projects, you set yourself up to complete them.

Habit #5 Pursuit of continuous learning.

The fifth habit is to pursue continuous learning. Block time off in your calendar to learn something new every day. We can never afford to stop learning. When we stop learning, we stop growing. Never get comfortable in your current state of knowledge. Decide to be a continuous learner the rest of your life and it will pay you great dividends. The people who develop at the expert level are the people who earn the higher wages. Study to become an expert in your field. Study by researching material on-line, learning from experts, obtaining certifications, or going back to school. Take advantage of the resources that are at your fingertips. Ask your employer to pay for that certification that you want so that you become an expert. Lobby for yourself and show your employer that paying for your certification, class(es) or school makes you a better performer and helps you meet team and company objectives. If you end of paying for the training, you are worth the investment.

> *"Never get comfortable in your current state of knowledge."*

Habit #6 Tell your story.

Habit number six is to always be ready to tell your story. When you share the right story at the right time, opportunities become available. Every great story has three components: 1) what the situation was (e.g., we needed to accomplish XYX) 2) what the struggle was (e.g., we had ABC obstacles and we had a deadline) 3) the remedy you provided (I came up with the plan on how to accomplish XYZ) and the resolution (e.g., the plan I devised worked and we accomplished XYZ, we accomplished it on time and senior management was incredibly pleased). In summary, start your conversation with the workplace situation, you tell them what the struggle was; share the remedy you provided and finally, what the result was. Always be ready to share a story where you stood out and solved a workplace problem.

The six habits of powerful people are about developing the habits and hard work that lead to successful outcomes. Consistently perform these habits every day and week. When you develop these habits, you will experience greater personal satisfaction, successes, and rewards.

> *"The six habits of powerful people are about developing the habits and hard work that lead to successful outcomes."*

PRINCIPLE #2 – How to Leverage Your Personality

I am excited to share principle number two with you about personalities and how to leverage them. Do we understand our personalities and how to leverage them? When we understand our personalities, we understand how we convey ourselves and then we can lean into them and use them to our advantage. When you understand your personality and the personality of those you connect with, you can improve your relationships and your workplace successes. Oftentimes, we clash with colleagues at work because we do not understand our personality nor their personality. This is why I highly recommend that you take personality tests. When you take these tests, relax and do not overthink it. I have a couple of tests I want to share with you. When you take these personality tests, have fun! Also, do not try to make yourself "look good" when taking these tests. Your personality and all of our personalities have good qualities (strengths) and different qualities (I won't call them bad). Enjoy the process of learning more about yourself. When you get the results, embrace yourself you and your own personality. The great news is that these tests are not expensive and taking the test will be rewarding. My colleagues and I took a personality test during a time when we were being mentored by our senior leaders. The personality test we took is called, "Insights Discovery – Color Personality Test." The idea behind this personality measurement, is that most of us, if not all of us, have a dominant personality type, expressed in one of four colors. The personality types are: 1) fiery red, 2) sunshine yellow, 3) cool blue and 4) earth green.

Please note that one personality type is not better than another.

I will give you the definition of the colors just as a "cheat" sheet or insight into what you can expect when your personality type is revealed. The first color in this personality test is fiery red. Red personality types are extravert thinkers.

When your test results reveal that your personality type is "***Fiery Red***," your attributes are:

Competitive, Demanding, Determined, Strong-willed, Purposeful.

The fiery red personality's mantra is: "Be Brief, Be Bright, Be Gone".

My primary personality type is fiery red. When you are talking to me at work, I want you to get to the point. My 2nd dominant color is yellow –that's the side of me that likes to be social. After taking Insights Discovery – Color Personality Test," I was able to spot other red personality types fairly quickly. This happened one time during our annual Christmas work party. Our senior leaders provided a breakfast spread. We dressed up in our favorite holiday attire. When we arrived, all the food was laid out and served to each of us by our senior leadership. Whenever we had our year-end party, there was always a short program near the end. Our company would sponsor a local charity and present them with a gift. We would celebrate our charitable gifting with a presentation. In this one year, the organizers of this party decided it would be great if we had two colleagues play their instruments as part of the presentation. Our CIO, Ben, was sitting front and center at the program, wearing a Santa hat. The program was going just as it always had. The presentation to our selected charity was ending, so Ben sprung from his chair to give his closing remarks. However, Katie jumped on the mic instead. Katie announced that our beloved colleague musicians, Michael and Logan were going to perform for us. We all applauded and Ben sat back down. Michael and Logan played their instruments. Michael played a song and then Logan. We all clapped with enthusiasm. Ben rose from his chair again to give his closing remarks, only to learn that Michael and Logan were not done; he returned to his chair. Michael played another selection and so did Logan. We all clapped with enthusiasm. Once again, Ben rose from his chair to give his closing remarks, but Michael and Logan were not done. Ben once again took his chair. I watched him during this entire process. I glanced over at him and his temperament had changed. It was clear that his patience was running out. I am certain that he enjoyed the music, but the program was just too long. By this time, instead of looking like a cheerful Santa wearing a Santa hat, he was starting to look like the Grinch. I watched his body language as he painfully sat through the next three selections. It was clear that he was doing everything in his power to sit through whatever was the remaining number of songs. Finally, Katie came back. We clapped again for Michael and Logan. Our CIO was now able to give his closing remarks. The truth was, this program was too long for him. He wanted this program to "Be Brief, Be Bright and Be Gone," but he suffered through it. Few people realized what was going on with him, but thanks to my newly found ability to recognize personalities, I was aware of his discomfort. Several days later I saw Ben at a meeting. After the meeting ended, I asked him if he had taken the Insights Discovery – Color Personality Test. He said he had. I asked, "Are you the red personality type?" He answered, "Yes, I am." Because I had developed a rapport with him, we laughed about how he fared at the Christmas party.

In review, we said the red personality traits are: Competitive, Demanding, Determined, Strong-willed, Purposeful. Does this personality sound like anyone you know? Whatever your color personality, it is important not to try to change who you are. Embrace who you are! Whatever your personality is, be sensitive to how the other color personality types are experiencing you.

Let's move on to the sunshine yellow personality type:
Sunshine Yellow *is:*
Sociable, Dynamic, Demonstrative, Enthusiastic, Persuasive.
Sunshine Yellow personality's mantra is: "Involve Me".

There is a person on our team at work that is "yellow" and so she is sociable. We can count on her to throw all the fun office parties. The yellow personality types are strongly extroverted, radiant, and friendly. This is my second dominate personality type.

The personality type cool blue is the third personality type:
Cool Blue *is:*
Cautious, Precise, Deliberate, Questioning, Formal.
Their mantra is: "Give Me the Details."

The cool blue personality types are task-oriented introvert thinkers. People with the blue personality want to think before they talk. They are analytical. They like preparing and organizing their thoughts.

The fourth personality type is earth green.
Earth Green *is:*
Caring, Encouraging, Sharing, Patient, Relaxed.
Their mantra is: "Show Me You Care."
The green personality types want others to be able to rely on them. They focus on relationships and values.

Research has proven that highly successful people are self-aware. This is a common strait that highly successful people share. This is a treasure you gain from taking personality tests. Taking the right personality tests help us to be self-aware.

I would like to recommend one more test for you. It is called the DISC personality test. The DISC test model measures behavior in terms of four tendencies:
- D – dominance
- I – Influence
- S – Steadiness
- C – Conscientiousness

You can get you own DISC General Characteristic Report at: resourcesunlimited.com>solutions>The Five Behaviors>Five Behaviors Personal Development Profile.

The DISC General Characteristics Report Includes:
- Behavioral Highlights
- Behavioral Overview
- Motivating Factors
- Strategies For Increased Effectiveness
- Demotivating Factors

Understanding your personality helps you to know why you respond the way you do and what your tendencies are, both good and bad. We must be aware and manage our personalities because they impact our relationships with other people, including our colleagues, significant others, bosses, spouses, children, etc.

Both the "Insights Discovery – Color Personality Test" and DISC are great tools. The results from these tests help you to leverage your greatness and to be on guard for your weaknesses. Therefore, take time to learn your personality type. Then seek to understand those around you as well. Life is all about relationships, and if there is one person we need to understand and know well it is ourselves. Then seek to understand those around you as well. Knowing your personality type is key to enhancing your power in the workplace.

PRINCIPLE #3 – How to Cultivate Your Strengths

Oftentimes we have superpowers within us that lie dormant because we do not realize they exist. Your natural talents are your superpowers, that is your strengths. You may possess strengths like, being a deliberator, activator, relator or sense of the future. Too often we focus on our weaknesses and do not develop our strengths. Gallup scientists have discovered through years of research that people have several times more potential for personal advancement and growth when they invest energy into developing their strengths instead of correcting their deficiencies.

I shared previously with you how I knew as a little girl that one day television would not be free. I knew this because I have a strength or superpower called strategy. A few characteristics of this talent include:

1) Having the ability to accurately evaluate the best or right path to take. 2) When you are naturally strategic, you are able to simplify chaos. For many years I did not leverage this talent because I was not aware of its presence. When you don't know your superpowers, you don't tap into them and you don't advance yourself like you should. It was not until me and a group of colleagues took a Clifton Strengths Assessment that we found out about our unique strengths and how to lean into them.

Clifton Strengths is an on-line psychological assessment developed by Dr. Don Clifton, a world-renowned psychologist. Dr. Clifton invested 40 years of research on identifying human strengths. After all these years of research, thousands of interviews of people and analyzing of data, Clifton's research identified 34 themes of strength (talents). When you take the assessment, you will discover your top five strengths and best understand what makes you tick.

When you understand your strengths, you can align your natural talents with your purpose and best realize your goals.

When I received my assessment results, I was thrilled to learn my talents and better understood why I am the way I am. Here are my five top strengths revealed from this assessment:

1. Strategic
2. Achiever
3. Learner
4. Arranger
5. Activator

Below are a few examples of what the strategic and achiever talent sound like:

The Strategic Strength sounds like this:

"Somehow I knew the consequences of making that decision before anyone else did."

The Achiever Strength sounds like this:

"On my list of fifty-five things, I have already accomplished twenty of them. I am feeling so good about myself."

When you understand your strengths, you can align your natural talents with your purpose and best realize your goals.

The Gallup research says: successful people start with a dominant talent. Then they add skills, knowledge, and practice, and when they do this, that is when the superpower shows up. The raw talent serves as a multiplier. Here is the formula that results in you enhancing your natural power:

TALENT *(a natural way of thinking, feeling, or behaving)*

x **INVESTMENT** *(time spent practicing developing skills and building your knowledge base)*

___

STRENGTH *(the ability to consistently provide near-perfect performance)*

Too often people are not doing work that reflects their strengths and when people are not able to use their strengths, this is what happens:
- They dread going to work.
- They have more negative than positive interactions with colleagues.
- They treat customers poorly.
- They achieve less daily.

> ***"People have several times more potential for growth when they invest energy in developing their strengths instead of correcting their deficiencies."***

Further, research by Clifton Strengths confirmed that when people get to focus on their strengths every day, they are six times as likely to report having an excellent quality of life in general.

Below I share a little more about the type of talents.

There are four domains of strengths/talents: 1) Executing, 2) Influencing, 3) Relation Building and 4) Strategic Thinking. When you take the Clifton-strengths assessment, your top five strengths will reside within these domains.

Here they are:

1) Executing Talents

Achiever	Arranger	Belief	Consistency	Deliberative
Discipline	Focus	Responsibility	Restorative	

2) Influencing Talents

Activator	Command	Communication	Competition
Maximizer	Self-Assurance	Significance	Woo

3) Relationship Building

Adaptability	Connectedness	Developer	Empathy	Harmony
Includer	Individualization	Positivity	Relator	

4) Strategic Thinking

Analytical	Context	Futuristic	Ideation
Input	Intellection	Learner	Strategic

Colleges are starting to use these assessments during the admissions process to help students identify their strengths. I recommend an assessment like this that helps you identify what you are strong in. When you know what you are strong in, it will serve you well in your purpose, work life and personal life.

Below is the link to the assessment. I'd like to encourage you to get it done whether you are in the workplace or heading to college. When you understand your strengths, you will know how to channel your efforts.

Visit www.gallup.com> Top 5 CliftonStrengths

"When you know what you are strong in, it will serve you well in your purpose, work life and personal life."

PRINCIPLE #4 – How to Crack the People Puzzle & Manage Conflicts

Crack the People Puzzle

We all want to successfully lead others and to do so, we need to crack the people puzzle. We crack the people puzzle by mastering some key skills including:

1. Interpersonal Skills
2. Growth in emotional intelligence
3. Effective communication
4. Ability to show empathy

Interpersonal Skills

Interpersonal skills are indicators of how well you relate and communicate with others. And building great relationships at work is vital. We all need great interpersonal skills in the workplace. Develop good relationships with your employees, your manager and your manager's boss. In order to cultivate these relationships, there are two extremely important interpersonal skills you need to cultivate: 1) building good rapport and 2) the ability to read others' body language. Building good rapport has to do with taking the time to get to know your employees, bosses and senior leadership personally. The Oxford Languages defines rapport as a close and harmonious relationship in which the people or groups concerned understand each other's feelings or ideas and communicate well. In order to build rapport, you must spend time with the people you're leading, your manager and other stakeholders. This involves getting outside of yourself, listening and sharing personally. You need to spend time with them in a 1:1 setting, building trust and listening. When you are leading other people, avoid a cookie cutter style of management. Secondly, during these conversations, pay particular attention to their body language cues. They may be saying one thing, but their body language is communicating something entirely different. Body language responses are a far more accurate than verbal responses.

Valuable interpersonal skills include:
- *Building good relationships*
- *Ability to read body language and facial expressions (non-verbal)*
- *Gaining and keeping people's attention while you speak*
- *Practicing active listening*
- *Being charismatic*
- *Finding common ground with others – great method for*

diffusing conflicts

- *Having high emotional empathy – being able to read the needs of others*
- *Building trust*
- *Looking to learn from every encounter with people*

Maya Angelou said, "I've learned that people will forget what you said, people will forget what you did, but people will never forget how you made them feel."

Whether you are leading a team, in a 1:1 with a supervisor or a heart to heart with your boss or colleague, receiving and giving feedback is important. One good practice to do is before you leave their presence ask them if they feel that they have been heard. Then, do not be quick to talk if they are quiet. Give them an opportunity to give you feedback. Then, you need courage to ask this, but ask them "How can I improve?" When you are giving feedback to your employees, make sure they understand what is expected of them. Give the feedback, they need to develop and set up a unique development plan for each of your direct reports. And give them effective and timely feedback. If you see an opportunity for an individual to grow, do not wait until the end of the year to share that feedback. If you see an opportunity to give feedback near term, give it to them.

When giving feedback, give a compliment of something they have done well. Let them know that we are all learning and working to improve, including me. Ease into the other feedback, which are opportunities for personal growth. Feedback gives people the opportunity to tweak things and improve.

When you are managing people, you want to do these things:
1. *Be real - be authentic*
2. *Be an active listener*
3. *Praise and give rewards*

4. Show them that you care
5. Be trustworthy

"Interpersonal skills are indicators of how well you relate and communicate with others."

Emotional Intelligence

Emotional intelligence is key to having great relationships with your teams, colleagues and bosses. Emotional intelligence is defined as skill in perceiving, understanding and managing emotions and feelings (per Dictionary.com). Emotional intelligence is about getting in touch with your emotions and using them to work for you and not against you. To be successful in managing people and relationships in general, you need to understand how you and your emotions influence you and the people around you. Emotional intelligence means you understand the following:

1. Knowing the real you and how you respond to people and events
2. Knowing how to successfully manage your emotions
3. Knowing how to successfully manage your interactions with others
4. Understanding other people's emotions in real time

The key to all of this is to manage yourself and your emotions and not let your emotions manage you. According to "Emotional Intelligence 2.0," "Since our brains are wired to make us emotional creatures, your first reaction to an event is always going to be an emotional one. The physical path for emotional intelligence starts in the brain at the spinal cord. Your primary senses enter here and must travel to the front of your brain through the limbic system (where you feel things) before you can think rationally about your experience." Thus, men and women are equally impacted by emotions and if we don't manage our emotions, our first reaction to an event will be emotional.

Knowing the real you and how you respond to people and events

People who are high performers know themselves for who they are. They understand how they respond to people and events, so that they can control the outcomes. You also can control the outcomes that impact you emotionally by performing the following:

- Be open – share who you are (not all of your business but share some things)
- Paying attention to your emotions and how you respond to people
- Recognize triggers which include people or things that push your buttons
- Observe how you behave under pressure
- Pay attention to how your body responds to people, stress and other events
- Observe how your emotions impact other people
- Ask other people you trust how they are affected by your emotions

To know how to successfully manage your emotions, here are a few tips:

- Think happy thoughts.
- Slow your roll and give your brain time to process before you respond.
- Write down the people and events that push your buttons. Be aware.
- Practicing breathing exercises.

Knowing how to successfully manage your interactions with others
- Respect people and value them.

- Don't wear your feelings on your sleeve - meaning remain open to the opinions of others and hear them out. It does not mean you agree but at least listen and look for common ground in discussions.

- Be adaptable – which is always a mindset to live by.

- Allow people to share their perceptions of you.

- Propose to have an open mind – steer away from being defensive.

- Live in the moment.

- Make eye contact with whoever is speaking.

- Learn how to "pal up" not suck up.

- Genuinely appreciate the opinions of others.

Understanding other people's emotions in real time
- Learn to read body language including reading the eyes of the person you're talking to.

- Treat people how they want to be treated.

Effective Communication -
Communicating with different personality types

Chances are you heard effective communication is necessary to lead a team, but you may not have heard how to do it. Effective communication begins with honestly learning your team members; how they are wired, learning their personalities and their strengths. As we've said earlier, every person's personality has great attributes as well as not so great, or areas to avoid or improve. We also discussed how to leverage your own personality and how to recognize your own strengths. It was necessary to introduce these self-discovery opportunities first. Before you can truly learn someone else, you need to have a decent handle on understanding yourself.

We previously discussed the "Insights Discovery – Color Personality Test" and talked about each of the color-coded personality traits. We said there is one color associated with each of the four personality types and that every person typically has one dominant personality type or trait. Those personality types again are:

Fiery Red: their mantra is "Be brief, Be bright, Be gone"
Sunshine Yellow: their mantra is "Involve Me"
Cool Blue: their mantra is "Give Me Details"
And Earth Green: their mantra is "Show Me You Care"

Their verbal styles are as follows:
Fiery Red- Fast pace
Sunshine Yellow – Expressive
Cool Blue – Formal, reserved
Earth Green – Steady and informal

When it comes to recognizing your teams' personalities, I am providing a "cheat sheet" that you can use to recognize the personality types on your team. Once you identify their individual personality types, you can more effectively communicate with them and assign work based on their personalities.

Let's say you have a direct report, boss, C-suiter or colleague that is a *Fiery Red* personality.

The fiery red personality is purposeful, competitive, determined and demanding.

More facts about the "fiery" red personality include – they are:
- Extraverted in thinking
- Fast paced and decisive

- Focused on the tasks and getting results
- Can be impatient and blunt
- Can seek security by being in control

Strategies for leading and adapting to the fiery red personality include:

When approaching them – be brief and direct, not hesitant
When questioning them –
    look out for impatience; follow their pace
When presenting before them – be well-organized and factual
When handling objections –
    meet their resistance with reflective questions

Take a look at these attributes again. There is a reason why they are "fiery" red. Fiery red individuals prefer work that challenges them and holds their attention. Their value-add to the team is their force of energy and their willingness to take risks. If you are leading a fiery red personality, help them channel what they are great at. They are great communicators that revel in taking on challenging work and opportunities.

Fiery red personality - potential areas to watch out for include:
- They can lack empathy.
- They can be unaware of others' feelings.
- They can over-control the situation.

The key is to understand your team individually and collectively, recognizing the contrasts in personalities.

Let's say you have a direct report, boss, C-suiter or colleague that is a *Sunshine Yellow* personality.

The sunshine yellow personality is sociable, enthusiastic and demonstrative.

Facts about the sunshine yellow personality – they are:

- Friendly and personable
- Fast paced and spontaneous
- Focused on interaction and relationships
- Outgoing
- Irritated by boredom
- Likes recognition

Strategies for leading and adapting to the sunshine yellow personality include:

When approaching them – be sociable, focus on them

When questioning them – don't give too many details

When presenting before them –

tell stories and focus on benefits in the future

When handling objections from them –

ask questions that will allow them to express themselves

When a team member is sunshine yellow, speak to them in an enthusiastic and upbeat fashion, and be personally interested in them. They can be chatty, so let them speak. Their value adds to the team are optimism and ability to engage and involve people. Engage your sunshine yellow personality for ideas on how to bring the team together. This should be your "go to" person for employee social events as they excel in this. They love praise and they love bringing their ideas to the table. Their goal is popularity and approval.

Potential areas to watch out for include:
- They sometimes can be sarcastic.
- They sometimes overestimate their own abilities.
- They sometimes overestimate the abilities of others.

Next, let's discuss the *Cool Blue* personality. Here are some things that can help you engage with the cool blue personality on your team.

Understand that they are: formal, questioning, cautious and precise. To build a rapport with the cool blue personality:
- Be structured and clear.
- Offer up details that meet their requirements.
- Do not pressure them.
- Give them time to think.
- Offer to follow up in a formal matter, e.g. email

Strategies for leading and adapting to the cool blue personality:

When approaching them –

slow down and be more formal, not too direct

When questioning them –

be methodical and structured, take notes

When presenting before them – be ready to show proof

When gaining commitment – provide logical alternatives

When work calls for details and analytics, give that work to the cool blue personality. They will get it done. Cool blues are great observers that possess a high depth of critical perception. They have a preference to draw their conclusions based on the facts. When you are presenting ideas, they are the ones that may ask you for a chart or more details surrounding your decision. They prefer written communication. They are introverted, but that does not mean they are unfriendly. Their value-add to the team is precision, consistency and organization.

Cool blue personality - potential areas to watch out for include:
- Having to prompt them to move on things at a faster pace
- Having to encourage them to take more risks – to embrace uncertainty

Last, but certainly not least, is the personality, *Earth Green.*

The earth green personality is caring, sharing, encouraging, relaxed and patient.

Here are facts about the earth green personality – they are:
- Introverted feeling
- Wants to be liked
- Slow and easy in style
- Casual and conforming
- Irritated by insensitivity

Strategies for leading and adapting to the earth green include:

When approaching them – talk slower and be more open

When questioning them – ask their opinion, show personal interest

When presenting before them – get feedback and quote benefits

When handling objections –

don't push, check carefully to reveal concerns

To build a rapport with the earth greens:
- Use less emotion in your voice.
- Be easy-going and non-pressuring.
- Slow down when talking to them and take your time.
- Be supportive and considerate.

It is important that you be a good listener with earth greens. The earth green personality type is: caring, encouraging, willing to share, patient, relaxed. The earth green personality's mantra is: "Show Me You Care." When you have an earth green personality that you lead or collaborate with, you need to show them how their work or your team's work is helping others. They believe in maintaining harmony. Their value adds to the team include their empathy that they show others and attentive listening. The greens are great team members and are great for customer facing roles. But earth green personalities can also be indecisive. They can vacillate on decisions. And when they are the decision makers, they need help to stick with the plan or decision. They want your support and encouragement.

Earth green personality - potential areas to watch out for include:
- Under pressure, they may feel overburdened.
- They may fear confrontation.
- They can be indecisive.

Show Empathy

Empathy is your ability to understand and share in the feelings of another person. It simply says put yourself in the other person's shoes to better understand him or her and to communicate better. Ask yourself, 'if I were him, how would I feel if that situation happened to me in a meeting?'

Also, show you care with words of affirmation.

How to Manage Conflict

Conflict is something we all inevitably must deal with in all our relationships, including in the workplace. However, there are practical things we can do to resolve conflict. The main objective in resolving conflict is to cause the other person to feel understood. You must prepare your heart, manage your tone, and have a vision of your desired outcome. Before you have a difficult conversation, you need to visualize in your mind that this conversation will go well. You want to think of this person you're going to meet with, with a heart of empathy. You also want to speak with a calm tone. Decide to listen more and talk less, and do not try to defend your perspective. Instead, listen for their perspective. Once you hear their perspective you want to repeat (echo) back what they said, even if it is negative. When you echo back what the other person said, they feel understood. The idea is not to argue with their point of view, but just to repeat it. When you repeat their point of view, ask them, "Is this correct?" When they say, "yes," they will experience a chemical reaction in their brain, called oxytocin. Oxytocin is a hormone that makes people feel like they are bonding with you. Do not shy away from repeating negative things they have said during this discussion. For example, if your team member feels like you did not address their concern, you could say, "Do you feel like I did not address your concern?" Your team member will answer with "yes" or "correct." The minute they acknowledge your response with a yes or correct, oxytocin is released in their brain.

Another thing you want to do during the discussion is to warn them when you are going to give them bad news by saying, "I am sorry I have to share this…" Be sure to end the conversation on a positive note: e.g., "thanks so much for our talk." Propose to find common ground with that person, as this builds rapport.

In summary, here are the keys to managing conflict:
- *Be genuine.*
- *Stay calm, manage your emotions.*
- *Find your common interests / common ground.*
- *Show empathy and discuss your differences.*
- *Ask clarifying questions.*
- *Monitor the tone of your voice.*
- *Listen to understand them.*
- *Echo back what you heard.*
- *Give affirmations of their value before giving unpleasant feedback.*
- *Learn to receive and ask for feedback.*
- *If it is needed, apologize e.g. "I apologize if I offended you."*
- *Warn when bad news is coming by starting your sentence with "I'm sorry…"*

- *Do not interrupt them – if too many interruptions, they will shut down.*

- *Watch your body language because it needs to match your words.*

- *Pay attention to their body language – this will let you know how well it is going.*

What to do when people are upset

When people are upset, they do not feel understood:
1. *Have a private discussion with them.*
2. *Make sure you stay calm.*
3. *Watch the tone of your voice.*
4. *Listen to understand them.*
5. *Echo back what you heard.*
6. *Give affirmations.*
7. *If they are right, tell them.*

Cracking the people puzzle requires personal time and interest invested in others. To truly understand our employees and other stakeholders, it requires mastering of interpersonal skills, emotional intelligence, effective communication and ability to show empathy. Also, we cannot run away from conflict. Use these keys to manage and diffuse conflict, including managing your tone and deciding to listen more.

PRINCIPLE #5 – How to Engage Your Personal Brand

Personal branding is key to success in your career. Although this topic can make or break your career, there seems to be little discussion of it in corporate America. There can be many definitions for personal branding, but I like to keep it simple. Personal branding is what you are known for. If I were to ask you what are you known for? what would you say?

To be successful with personal branding, you want to make some important moves. So, let's get started – here are four important moves you need:

1. **Invest in yourself.**

    A part of successful personal branding involves solidifying your credibility. To be known for those things you want to be known for it is going to require personal investment. Take the time to invest in yourself financially to develop your skills. That may require more training, certifications or going back to school. The good news is that many employers will pay for these skills if you can justify that those investments will add value to you performing your work (current or future). Go ahead, put in the work and training that will solidify your credibility and your brand.

2. **Be your authentic self.**

    When it comes to personal branding, it is very important that you be your authentic self. Follow your trust meter, but if you want to be relatable, you need to be authentic. We connect best with others when they are real, and people will connect with you when you are real. I heard a story recently about a group of young professionals on a panel giving advice at a seminar. One of those professionals on the panel was very guarded and only spoke with corporate jargon. Needless to say, feedback from the participants about him was not good.

3. **Be likeable.**
   Being likeable is not about being phony, it's about being pleasant to experience you or be around you. Some of the traits of likeability include, being considerate, being a great listener and being able to effectively give and receive feedback.

4. **Have a great work ethic.**
   If your manager or colleagues were questioned about your work ethic, what would they say? Are you considered a hard worker? Being a hard worker does not mean you don't have a life. A hard worker should definitely have a healthy work/life balance.

5. **Manage perceptions.**
   There are times when you may be out of touch with what people's perceptions are of you. When it comes to personal branding, you want to know the perceptions people have of you. Other people's perceptions do not necessarily mean you are doing anything wrong, and this is not a call to action to change who you are. Instead, this is just a call to action to get the information to help you measure perceptions and possibly clear up misunderstandings.

6. **Define Your Brand**
   In defining your brand, ask yourself some questions, including:
   a. How do I view myself?
   b. How do I wish to be viewed in my organization and my industry?
   c. How does my brand and the company's brand align?

The Johari Window model

There is a tool you can use to collect feedback from others to gauge their perceptions of you and your brand. It is called the Johari Window model. The Johari Window model is great for gauging perceptions and improving self-awareness.

Here are the instructions for how to use the Johari Window to understand people's perceptions of your brand.

1. Grab a group of colleagues (or friends) to participate in this exercise with you. Each participant will receive a copy of "Johari Window Adjectives List" shown below. The person wanting the feedback (receiving insights) will choose 12 adjectives from the list of adjectives that best describe themselves. The other participants will each choose 8 adjectives that best describe the individual receiving the feedback/insights.

2. Then have each participant reveal one adjective they feel represents the individual (e.g, you) being assessed. Ask the individual (you)receiving the feedback if the adjective was on her list; if it is, place it in the "Open Self" box (see figure below). If it isn't, place it in the "Blind Self" box.

3. Continue sharing around the group, one by one, until there has been at least 10 open adjectives shared/listed.

4. The individual receiving the feedback/insights is then asked to reveal any remaining adjectives that have not yet been identified by participants. It may be that an individual identified the adjective, but the sharing process ended before they shared the adjective. If this happens add it to the "Open Self" box. If no one has an adjective that the individual receiving the feedback reveals, then it should be placed in the "Hidden Self" box.

Johari Window – below is a list of descriptors/adjectives.

Able	Giving	Powerful
Accepting	Happy	Private
Adventurous	Helpful	Proud
Aggressive	Humorous	Quiet
Assertive	Idealistic	Reflective
Autocratic	Impulsive	Relaxed
Autonomous	Independent	Reliable
Bold	Influential	Religious
Calm	Ingenious	Responsive
Caring	Innovative	Risk Taker
Cheerful	Inspirational	Searching
Clever	Intelligent	Self Aware
Complex	Introverted	Self Conscious
Compliant	Intuitive	Self Contained
Confident	Kind	Sensible
Courageous	Knowledgeable	Sentimental
Critical	Listener	Shy
Decisive	Logical	Silly
Demanding	Loving	Spiritual
Dependable	Loyal	Spontaneous
Dignified	Mature	Systematic
Diplomatic	Modest	Talkative
Dominating	Motivator	Tenacious
Empathetic	Nervous	Tense
Energetic	Observant	Thorough
Even-tempered	Open	Trustworthy
Extroverted	Organized	Warm
Flexible	Patient	Wise
Friendly	Persuasive	Witty

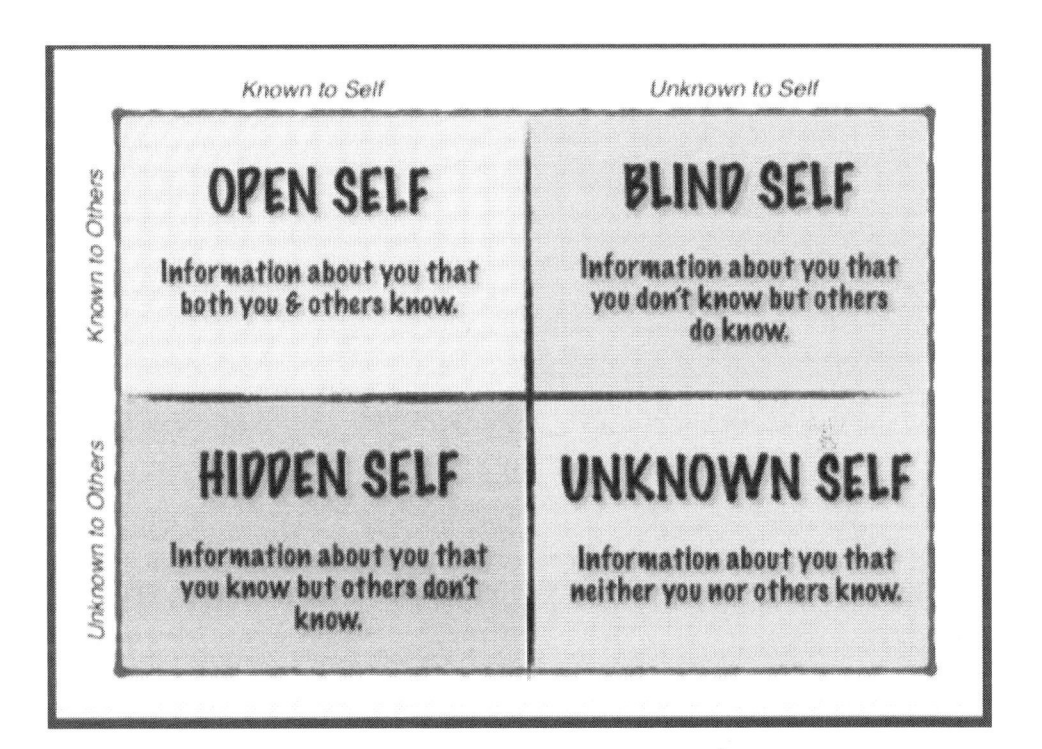

	Known to Self	Unknown to Self
Known to Others	**OPEN SELF** — Information about you that both you & others know.	**BLIND SELF** — Information about you that you don't know but others do know.
Unknown to Others	**HIDDEN SELF** — Information about you that you know but others don't know.	**UNKNOWN SELF** — Information about you that neither you nor others know.

After all the feedback has been received, here are some questions to ask of the participants:

1. What were the biggest surprises to you?
2. Which adjectives may be helpful to you since you now know others' perceptions, and observations?
3. What hidden adjectives would you like to show more often to your team members? What would be the first step you could take to move in this direction?

There is a simpler approach to apply the Johari Window method: Grab some colleagues, allow them to choose 8 adjectives from the list enclosed here. Choose 12 adjectives from the same list of adjectives to describe yourself. Have the colleagues share the adjectives they chose to describe you. Compare their adjective selections which the adjectives you chose to describe yourself. Then determine which of the categories the results landed in: Open self, blind self, hidden self or unknown self.

PRINCIPLE #6 – How to Conquer Your Blind Spots

We are all very familiar with physical blind spots. When we are on the road or expressway and we want to shift into another lane, we sometimes don't see a car is already occupying that lane and space we wanted to shift over to. Our mirrors may be perfectly aligned, but we still don't see that a car is there, because it is in our blind spot. Sometimes when it comes to our professional and personal relationships, we are operating with emotional blind spots that hinder us.

So, when we talk about emotional blind spots, what are they? Emotional blind spots are our inability to see our shortcomings or making the decision to ignore them. Basically, a blind spot is messing up emotionally without knowing it or refusing to work on it.

Most of the time, our emotional blind spots show up when we are communicating with colleagues in the workplace. Some common blinds spots include:

1. Not observing yourself objectively
2. Cutting people off without letting them finish
3. Avoiding difficult conversations
4. Being offended and not seeking help
5. Thinking negatively
6. Not being open to feedback

7. Miscommunication
8. Not believing in yourself

So how do we overcome these blind spots?

1. Increase our awareness and make decisions to objectively evaluate our behavior. Chances are, a boss, family member or colleague has already pointed out a blind spot we have. They may have repeatedly commented to us things like, "You cut me off while I was talking," or "let me finish." Instead of blowing people off, let's acknowledge those behaviors we should change.

2. Have the difficult conversations:
   - *Stay calm, manage your emotions.*
   - *Find your common interests / common ground.*
   - *Show empathy and discuss your differences.*
   - *Ask clarifying questions.*
   - *Monitor the tone of your voice.*
   - *Listen to understand them.*
   - *Echo back what you heard.*
   - *Pay attention to their body language – this will let you know how well it is going.*

3. Develop the habit of not being offended. Talk yourself into this. Say it as many times as you have to, "I am not easily offended" or "I choose to not be offended by …"

4. Practice being grateful. Neuroscience has proven that gratitude makes us feel good and helps to motivate us to accomplish goals. Gratitude positively shifts our thinking to enhance our well-be-

ing. This will help in reducing the blind spots because of positive thinking.

5. Think happy thoughts. Your attitude absolutely impacts your aptitude. When you are negative, it spills out in how you communicate with others.

6. Discipline your behaviors.

7. Be open to receive feedback and ask for it. You need to able to receive feedback and receive it well. I know it's not easy, but it is necessary. Giving and receiving feedback may help address some misconceptions. Be objective when evaluating the feedback you are receiving. If you know there is some truth in it, just make the adjustments and communicate the adjustments you made or are making with the appropriate audience.

8. Seek the advice of a trusted colleague, coaches, mentors, family or friends. Allow these trusted individuals to point out your blind spots. Listen to them and make the necessary adjustments.

9. Love yourself and be kind to yourself. You are SOMEBODY! You were made on purpose and with purpose.

10. Refuse to blame others for what's not going right. Do everything you can to make right choices and be successful.

11. Refuse to live a life of insolation. We need each other.

"Claiming that I don't need anyone is not a symbol of strength. It's a sign of dysfunction" - DAVID WINSTON

Implement the above actions to recognize your blind spots. This will create richer experiences in your relationships and your career.

PRINCIPLE #7 – How to Obtain the Optimal Work-life Balance

Sometimes we as professionals get so caught up in our work that we don't take care of ourselves. We spend so much time investing in companies with our resources and time, that we don't equally invest in self-care. I remember years ago being at work one day, and a colleague had a heart attack. They called an ambulance, sent flowers to his home and over the next couple of days, they divided up his work assignments amongst his team. Thankfully that colleague did recover and eventually returned to work, but my point is that your place of business will move on. If you become ill or die, they will find a way to get your job done without you. You and I may be replaceable in the workplace but we are not replaceable as human beings. That means we have to have enough self-respect and know our worth that we take care of ourselves first above everything else.

Setting boundaries

An important form of self-care is protecting ourselves from being mistreated by people. We teach people how to treat us by what we allow. Setting boundaries can protect your mental health and save you time.

Stop excessive outpouring to help others because when you do, you end up depleted, emotionally and physically exhausted. Some of these people are not adding value to your life. Do an inventory of the people you are rolling with. Get rid of energy draining, manipulating, selfish people, and be honest about the relationships you are in. On the other hand, you definitely need and want a few people (e.g. three to five) that you trust and you can share whatever you are going through.

Negative thoughts can hurt us and when it comes to thinking negative thoughts about people, no one is worth taking up real estate in our minds to constantly think about him or her. The best thing to do is to forgive those people. You can choose to forgive them. Say it repeatedly ("I forgive so and so") if you have to until you have really forgiven them. Our unforgiveness does not hurt them, but it can hurt us. Make a clean slate to forgive. Also let anger, bitterness, unforgiveness and resentment go!

Inner self-talk

What we think about affects us mentally, spiritually, and physically. There are life events and situations that we cannot control. However, we can control how we react to those events and situations. It may be tough, but we can reprogram how we think to live healthier and happier. Dr. Caroline Leaf in her book, "Switch on Your Brain" explains that, "As we think, we change the physical nature of our brain. As we consciously direct our thinking, we can wire out toxic patterns of thinking and replace them with healthy thoughts. (Then) we increase our intelligence and bring healing to our brains, minds, and physical bodies."

Physical care

One of the best ways to take care of yourself is in caring for your physical health. When we don't take care of our bodies it negatively impacts everything. Physical fitness helps us to reduce stress and to think clearly. It also gives us more energy. Exercise releases endorphins that release stress and pain. I can tell the difference between when I exercise regularly vs. when I sit on the couch. Exercise helps us to stay sharp in thinking, learning and judging. It can also help us lose weight, reduce heart disease and to manage our blood sugar levels.

Doctors are now prescribing patients to laugh as a way to reduce stress and provide natural healing to our bodies. Laughter helps to lower your blood pressure and improve our concentration. Also, smiling releases endorphins that help you to feel happier and to be more positive. There is a comedy called, "Rat Race" that I keep in my rotation of comedies to watch that make me laugh. I schedule laughter into my day so that I can be happier.

Even doing simple things as drinking enough water helps our bodies to function properly. When I was younger, I developed a habit of drinking one to two cups of coffee every day and I barely drank water. Unknowingly, as a result, I developed back pain and ended up taking an unplanned leave from work. My doctor was not able to figure out what was wrong. After weeks of not having any answers, my doctor ordered a test. To prepare for the test, I had to drink lots of water. What ended up happening was all that water moved throughout my body and flushed out kidney stones that me and my doctor were not aware existed. I immediately felt better. I experienced natural healing and I was soon able to return back to work. It was my lack of drinking water that was causing my health issues. Now I consistently drink 8 glasses of water a day just from that one life episode. So, drink water; it is a necessary part of good health. Do the things necessary to take care of your physical health.

Self-care at the workplace

You need to set boundaries at the workplace. There are several things you can do to take care of yourself in the workplace. You can plan out your week and spread your workload so that you don't feel burdened. You can also take care of heavier tasks earlier in the week to have a lighter week as you head into the weekend. Sometimes you need to say "no" to others and guard yourself from taking on too many things. Do not press yourself to change the world all in one day. Pace yourself and reward yourself for all of your accomplishments. Celebrate your small and big wins. Do not work through lunch, take breaks and get up from your work area. Go for a walk during breaks or lunch.

Another way to take care of yourself is to do breathing exercises. All you need to do is sit somewhere quietly for 10 minutes. Close your eyes. Put your hand on your stomach, inhale slowly for 10 seconds and exhale slowly for 10 seconds. You can do this breathing exercise anywhere.

Do the cool things outside of work that support your well-being while at work. This could include:

1. Learn a hobby
2. Do something fun
3. Ride a bike, hike, skate, walk, run
4. Travel
5. Pray, meditate, talk to God
6. Get a massage
7. Get your hair, nails or toes done
8. Live in the moment

You are your most important asset in the corporate world. Know your worth and take care of yourself above getting ahead in your career. Value yourself and ultimately do what is best for you.

CONCLUSION

The purpose of Girl, Boss Up! was to help you see your potential, find your purpose and expand your career. You are equipped with your personality, your personal brand, your strengths and your abilities. With just a little work, patience and perseverance, you will achieve your goals.

You're going to face challenges. Difficult bosses, uncomfortable corporate environments, discrimination, sexism, setbacks and conflict are all inevitable. You are going to make mistakes, and that's okay. What's important is that you learn from your mistakes, invest in yourself, grow and don't give up.

You have what it takes to win, so be your own unique self, continue to develop your talents and work them! Your advancement is directly connected to knowing your purpose, being in the right work spaces, developing your character and successfully managing your workplace relationships. Do what you're passionate about and what excites you, and do it with zeal and tenacity. Get in the right work assignments for you, grow and stay there until it's time to move to the next one.

Take care of yourself and don't let others push you off your square. Use what you've learned. Enjoy your personal journey and don't compare your journey to anyone else's. There is power in your abilities, and I am looking forward to your transformation of this world. Go do great things and don't look back. Go ahead, get ahead. Boss Up!

Made in the USA
Monee, IL
20 July 2021